Style Me Pretty
WEDDINGS

Style Me Pretty
WEDDINGS

INSPIRATION & IDEAS FOR AN UNFORGETTABLE CELEBRATION

ABBY LARSON

CLARKSON POTTER/PUBLISHERS
NEW YORK

CLARKSON POTTER is a trademark and POTTER
with colophon is a registered trademark of
Random House, Inc.

Library of Congress Cataloging-in-Publication Data
Larson, Abby.
Style me pretty weddings/Abby Larson.
—1st ed.   p.   cm.
1. Weddings.   2. Weddings—Planning.
3. Wedding etiquette.   I. Title.
HQ745.L37   2013
392.5—dc23
2012009451

ISBN 978-0-7704-3378-9
eISBN 978-0-7704-3380-2

Printed in China

PHOTOGRAPHY CREDITS APPEAR ON PAGES 248–50.
HAND CALLIGRAPHY BY Love, Jenna
BOOK DESIGN BY Laura Palese
COVER DESIGN BY Rachel Dlugos
COVER PHOTOGRAPHY: Jose Villa *(front, back top
and bottom)*; Sarah Yates *(back middle)*

1 3 5 7 9 10 8 6 4 2

First Edition

TO ALL OF THE

Brides

who find themselves awake at 2 A.M., Googling birdcage veils
and signature cocktail recipes. May this be a place of happy.
A celebration that you, my lovely, are getting married. To
the one you adore. And the wedding *will* be spectacular . . .
because he'll be standing up there waiting for you to say "I do."

Contents

Introduction

I CONFESS. I HAVE WHAT SOME MIGHT CALL

the best job in the entire world. As the founder of *Style Me Pretty*, a magazine-style blog that celebrates weddings in all of their forms and all of their fashions—from backyard beauties to million-dollar celebrations—I might be found on any given day surrounded by peonies, e-feasting on gilded cakes, tearing up while simultaneously oohing and ahhing at the myriad vows, toasts, and first dances that enter my in-box. Each has its own unique sense of style and grace. To date, our team has collectively blogged more than five thousand real weddings. Five thousand of the most pinch-me-perfect weddings a girl could ever wish for, with brides and grooms who are so madly in love, it nearly makes you blush.

And it's those very weddings that have inspired me to put every ounce of know-how that I have into the pages of this beautiful book: a book that overflows with never-been-seen-before ideas and inspirations, celebrations so breathtaking that you can hardly believe they were crafted by real brides, with real love—brides who value the thoughtful touches, the little moments of personality and spunk, the details that transform a pretty wedding into a bespoke wedding.

Brides . . . just like you.

My hope is that this book will become your inspiration bible, that through the pages and pages, chapters upon chapters of pretty, you will find that moment or that detail that will inspire your day. And I hope it will give you the confidence to design a wedding that is not only a hold-the-phone stunner but also one that is meaningful, filled with love, and a complete reflection of who you are as a couple.

This isn't your standard coffee-table book. Of course it's filled to the brim with the most steal-worthy, awe-inspiring eye candy a girl could ever want—images from some of the world's best artists and designers. But beyond the beauty, this book is also overflowing with practical, useful information that will make that thoughtfully designed wedding you've been eyeing . . . a reality. I'm talking brand-new events to inspire and excite you, blueprints that show you how to achieve the aesthetic that you've fallen for, and DIY projects that are mix and matchable to suit different wedding looks. This book is your very own style guide, a little piece of wedding heaven that you can tuck into your bag and carry with you to meetings with vendors, lunches with girlfriends, and late-night fridge-fests with your mom.

We hope that through the pages of this book you will find that same sense of raw beauty that you've found over the years on *Style Me Pretty*. These weddings and ideas were carefully chosen to show brides everywhere that classically trained perfection is not the benchmark for a flawless celebration. Instead, it's the layers upon layers of personality that always leave the longest-lasting impression. It's spunk paired with style. It's elegance paired with spontaneity. It's sophistication paired with laughs, love, and pure happiness that make for a truly epic fête.

This book, at its core, is about the details. It's about the little touches that add up to create the big picture. The very special somethings that make for the prettiest of pretty weddings, the most thoughtful of celebrations and events. And the simple fact that designing a bespoke wedding of your very own is not only possible . . . it's easy. And really fun.

So kick off your heels, grab a glass of bubbly, and prepare to lose yourself entirely in the pure beauty of weddings styled pretty.

The Anatomy
of a BESPOKE
Wedding

BESPOKE. IT'S THE WORD USED TO DEFINE SOMETHING that is custom designed just for you. A gown so stunning, so chic, it fits your every curve to perfection. A glittery gold ring that shines brightest when placed only upon your finger. Thoughtfully mixed signature cocktails, a stack of letterpress monogrammed stationery, a hand-drawn silhouette, a pair of just-worn-enough jeans. Bespoke is a sensibility. It's the idea that you can tailor the details of your life so that they sparkle just a bit more, so that your favorite things collide into one spectacularly unique equation built exclusively for you.

So what makes a wedding bespoke? Not the stiff, buttoned-up way that this rather traditional word implies. What will make it perfectly imperfect, unabashedly joyful, in a way that you have been craving since the moment you said "I will"?

Here, my lovelies, is my recipe. A bespoke wedding is an utterly unique design that could bring a style aficionado to tears. It's the lovingly chosen flowers, so pretty you wonder if they are real. It's you and your soon-to-be husband donning fabulous tradition-with-a-twist threads and your innate sense that no other wedding will ever be quite as great as your own. But most of all, it's the details. Details that are fun and spirited and full of soul. Details that mean everything to you and your other half, both exquisite and immensely personal. Add to that photography that will leave you breathless and, of course, crazy stupid love that pours out of each and every image. This, my friends, is a bespoke wedding.

To illustrate this very notion, I have chosen a single wedding that embodies everything that a bespoke celebration should be. A wedding that marries my favorite must-haves into one jaw-droppingly gorgeous affair. Above all else, one that is totally style-stamped for the couple behind the day. When you recover from the wedding euphoria that's sure to kick in after devouring the following example, I'll break it all down for you, piece by beautiful piece, showing you exactly how simple it is to craft a day that is oh-so-very-you. And more specifically, how you can use a real wedding like this one to inspire your own unparalleled celebration.

COUPLE'S NAME · Rachael & Justin—Floweree, MT
EVENT DESIGNER & FLORIST · Joy Thigpen **PHOTOGRAPHER** · Jose Villa Photography

---

1 DETERMINE YOUR COUPLE STYLE

Step

In the adventures of designing a memorable celebration, determining who you are as a couple is the first and most critical step. And it's the one step that too many newly engaged pairs forget to pay homage to. It's knowing that you both love curling up by the fire decked out in flannels, or that you come to life when donning your favorite cocktail ring or throwing back margaritas poolside. It's acknowledging that your home is styled primarily around the color blue because that's his favorite hue, or that you both thrive at a great party where sparkles are a requirement. Your Couple Style will guide your wedding planning, ensuring that every decision revolves around the ideas you love.

For Justin and Rachael, this first step may have been the easiest. Both lawyers living in Los Angeles, the couple wanted a wedding that evoked the sophistication of their city life with the homegrown tradition of their roots. Rustic Elegance, one of the most well-loved wedding styles around, suited this adorable couple to a T.

2
Step

DETERMINE THE *FEEL* OF YOUR WEDDING

Figuring out how you want your wedding to *feel* is an important component in determining your Couple Style. A wedding that is rustic and elegant, for example, can have many different vibes, from casual to formal, sweet to sophisticated. Finding the ambiance that represents you as a couple is so very necessary in the larger equation, and it will help you infuse your entire celebration with personal touches. Do you envision your day as intimate, with your own vows and family-style dining? Do you see a more celebratory vibe filled with dancing, toasts, and whimsical surprises? From the ceremony readings to the reception music, from the type of food that you choose to the lighting that you select, all of these layers can be crafted around the wedding *feel* that you have determined.

> **❝** *Having the wedding at such a personal location felt like inviting all of our guests into our home. We wanted everyone to be relaxed, comfortable, and, most important, to have a great time. We based a lot of the wedding on that idea and added in whimsical touches like a lemonade stand before the ceremony and late-night burgers, french fries, and milkshakes.* **❞**
> —RACHAEL, THE BRIDE

SPECIAL TIPS

• **A GREAT STARTING PLACE** is to dig out all of those old photos from the early days, when you and your fiancé were just getting to know each other. Trace your journey together. Relive the moments that you loved the most. Find the common thread. Perhaps it's dinners at the same neighborhood bistro. Late-night trips to the movie theater. Game nights with friends and family. Find the moments that bring you to life as a couple.

3 Step | NAIL DOWN A GORGEOUS VENUE

Choosing the right venue means that you are selecting the canvas onto which your wedding will be painted. Imagine hosting a rustic celebration in a modern loft. The recipe suddenly becomes disjointed, making it so much more challenging to articulate your vision. Instead, find a venue that will make your wedding style sparkle; this will elevate your vision to a place where execution suddenly becomes quite easy.

For Rachael and Justin, this could have been Step 1. They knew their celebration would be at Rachael's family farm in Montana, where her great-grandparents were the original homesteaders on the land and her grandmother now lives. Rachael even attended a one-room schoolhouse down the dirt road.

"Rachael really wanted to have the wedding under the cottonwood tree. All family photos were taken there and most of her life's major events were documented under that tree." —JOY

Step 4 · SOURCE INSPIRATION

Now it's time to find those details—to scour the Web, to hit the blogs, to uncover the images that reflect your ideas and your inspirations, and that will turn your canvas into something wildly special. The key to making your inspiration really work for you and to ensure that you aren't losing yourself amid all of the pretty is to stay organized, to source thoughtfully, and to learn to edit yourself along the way.

WE ARE SO CONVINCED that the first four steps—especially this one—are the most critical in laying down the proper foundation for your bespoke wedding that we've actually made this step into a mini-handbook.

From INSPIRATION *to* ORGANIZATION

YOUR GUIDE TO MANAGING ALL OF YOUR WEDDING MUST-HAVES . . . AND STAYING COMPLETELY SANE IN THE PROCESS

Inspiration can be found tucked into the smallest of corners or the largest of spaces. It can be discovered in the vastness of Central Park just as easily as it can be found in a single color within your favorite painting. And thanks to the millions of swoon-worthy ideas found online and in magazines, inspiration overload can come swiftly and without warning.

Not to fret. You are about to get a lesson in inspiration management, and these tools will ensure that you are on the path to wedding serenity. From teaching you how to organize your content both on- and offline to giving you ideas about distilling your many loves to execute your vision, this is your A–Z guide for staying calm and in control amid all of the pretty chaos. Let's get started.

STEP 1: SET YOURSELF UP RIGHT . . . FROM THE BEGINNING

Have one central location on your computer to store your online loves (*hint:* check out *SMP*'s "Favorites" file in your account dashboard). Creating categories and buckets to house your inspiration—the images you find on your favorite blogs, the color swatches you discover while scouring Pantone, the film clips from cinematographers, the color palettes on home décor sites, the gowns from your favorite designers—is a critical first step and will permit easy access to your ideas later down the road. You want to keep your major categories top level so that you don't start duplicating inspiration, making it much harder to find what you're looking for. For example, you'll need a folder for flowers, for invitations and paper goods, for dresses, for DIY ideas, etc. You can get more specific with your subfolders.

Here is an example of what your folder hierarchy might look like:

TOP LEVEL
Wedding Inspirations

SUBFOLDERS
Beauty / Bridesmaids / Décor / Fashion / DIY Projects / Flowers / Food and Drink / Groomsmen / Paper Goods / Music

SUB-SUBFOLDERS
Beauty: Eyes / Lips / Hair
Bridesmaids: Bridesmaid Dresses / Shoes / Jewelry / Gifts
Décor: Guest Books / Photo Booths / Décor Details / Chandeliers / Favor Displays
DIY Projects: Favors / Décor / Florals
Flowers: Centerpieces / Ceremony Florals / Reception Florals / Bouquet / Bouts
Food and Drink: App Ideas / Food Trucks / Signature Cocktails / Menu Ideas
Groomsmen: Tuxes / Bow Ties / Socks / Gifts
Paper Goods: Save the Dates / Invitations / Menus / Escort Cards / Programs
Music: Ceremony / Cocktail Hour / Reception

Now, this is only an example. Your folders will all depend on what you deem to be the most important elements of your wedding and your budget. The key is to stay as organized as possible online so that you can easily reference your ideas later on down the road.

CREATE A TRUSTY WEDDING BINDER. There is *no* online replacement to house things like beautiful fabric swatches, invitation samples, concept sketches, inspiring photographs, and beautiful ribbon . . . the elements that you have to *feel* to really love. Even if your planning tools and other traditional wedding binder accoutrements are online, simply fill an empty three-ring binder with sealable pouches, labeled as to what they contain.

WIELD YOUR SMARTPHONE. A notebook and a digital camera would work, too. Say you see an amazing centerpiece at a restaurant or a gorgeous textile while shopping. Perhaps you spot the perfect shade of pink on the cover of a book or an idea for your dessert table while grabbing a quick bite. You want to have a quick and dirty way to take a snapshot, e-mail it to yourself, and add it to your online inspiration file—which will be oh-so-perfectly organized thanks to your superhandy filing system.

STEP 2: DEFINE AND REFINE YOUR COUPLE STYLE

We mentioned earlier in the book that determining your Couple Style makes it so much easier to plan a wedding that is uniquely you—and that it's actually really, really easy (with a bottle of wine or your favorite tunes on in the background, it's also really fun). But we wanted to dive in a little deeper with you. Here are some of our favorite ways to really capture the spirit of your Couple Style:

- **Raid your closet** to discover the color palettes that you love, the silhouettes that you gravitate toward, the textures and the styles of clothing that you wear.

- **Write down a list** of your favorite songs, your favorite restaurants, your favorite recipes—the beloveds that turn your heart aflutter.

- **Visit potential venues,** such as barns and lofts, ballrooms and art galleries, to see where you feel the most inspired.

- **Hit up local farmers' markets** and art fairs to find ideas for color palettes, flower choices, and menu ideas.

- **Pull out your old CDs,** crank up the radio, and make it a date to check out local bands to determine the music styles you sway the best to.

- **Take our style quiz** and make the process that much easier.

Yep, we've come up with one very unscientific quiz, opposite, that will help you to find your own unique voice. Remember, Wedding Style, in all of its eclectic glory, is made to be mix and matched, so if your answers are all over the place, don't worry for even a second. It's that very combination of ideas that makes for a truly personal, truly layered affair.

Style Us Pretty QUIZ

1. **Your foolproof plan for date night involves**
   a. fireside cuddling complete with s'mores.
   b. a trusted classic—dinner and a movie.
   c. miniature golf and sushi.
   d. a hike in the great outdoors followed by a picnic for two.
   e. getting your art on at a new gallery opening and cocktails at your favorite local hot spot.

2. **Your must-have shoes that totally embody your style are**
   a. perfectly worn-in cowboy boots.
   b. classic black heels.
   c. sparkly, bow-dazzled ballerina flats.
   d. bohemian sandals that let your toes feel the open air.
   e. patent leather stilettos with a rhinestone platform.

3. **They say the dining room is the window to the soul. Not really, but in this case, it's the window to your wedding style. How do you choose to eat, drink, and be merry?**
   a. I like to belly up to a lovely, old farmhouse table.
   b. I prefer a formal dining room fit for the grandest of dinner parties.
   c. I feel most at home surrounded by an eclectic mix of chairs.
   d. What dining room? I opt to take my meals in the garden, dining under the stars.
   e. Think metal, Lucite, and all things sleek, and you're on the right track.

4. **My jewelry box is a sea of**
   a. lovely antique brooches from my grandmother.
   b. diamond studs and a pearl necklace or two.
   c. huge cocktail rings—the bolder the better.
   d. gold and rosewood bracelets.
   e. modern, geometric shapes and loads of bangles.

5. **How do you take your coffee?**
   a. With cream and sugar in a mason jar mug and a slice of apple pie on the side.
   b. Coffee?!? No, thank you. I prefer Earl Grey sipped from gorgeous fine china.
   c. A steaming Vanilla Latte in a polka-dot travel mug.
   d. In a vintage gold-rimmed cup found on a recent flea-market hunt.
   e. Double espresso in a handleless glass mug.

6. **It's vacation time. Where can we find you unwinding?**
   a. Enjoying the simple pleasures of life on a ranch in Wyoming, no laptops or iPhones in sight.
   b. Strolling the Champs-Élysées in the springtime.
   c. Dancing in the streets of Buenos Aires.
   d. Sipping vino in the Italian countryside.
   e. Lounging poolside at an ultracool boutique hotel in Los Angeles.

7. **Who is your ultimate style girl crush?**
   a. Taylor Swift
   b. Anne Hathaway
   c. Zooey Deschanel
   d. Sienna Miller
   e. Alexa Chung

8. **When you envision your wedding, the colors that come to mind are**
   a. neutrals with a dash of metallic.
   b. black and white.
   c. a mix of bright colors and patterns.
   d. green, green, and more green.
   e. monochromatic for a bold look.

9. **The mani/pedi style that best describes you:**
   a. A barely-there shade of pink.
   b. Classic red.
   c. You haven't met a shade of neon nail polish that you don't adore.
   d. A French mani/pedi for that pretty take on the au naturel look.
   e. Ombré nails in shades of gray.

CONTINUED . . .

10. When the weather is chilly, you opt for

    a. an ever-so-cozy, chunky wool sweater.

    b. a tailored peacoat.

    c. a cheeky cape in a bold hue.

    d. a faux fur vest.

    e. a leather motorcycle jacket.

11. We're talking favorite flora. What kind of flower girl are you?

    a. Olive branches and lavender have that rustic simplicity that I so adore.

    b. Nothing but fluffy, gorgeous peonies for this classic lady.

    c. I love the pop of a yellow billy ball.

    d. An effortless mix of fresh-picked wildflowers sets my heart aflutter.

    e. I go crazy for all things succulent.

12. Your correspondence style involves

    a. a handwritten note on vintage postcards.

    b. monogrammed and letterpressed—the only way you roll.

    c. watercolor note cards that add a dash of personality.

    d. sweet nothings scribbled on recycled stationery.

    e. anything printed in your favorite font: Helvetica.

13. If you had to pick a favorite romantic movie, it would be

    a. *Legends of the Fall*

    b. *Casablanca*

    c. *Amélie*

    d. *Mamma Mia*

    e. *Love Actually*

14. Close your eyes and imagine your dreamiest of future homes. What do you see?

    a. A ranch-style house surrounded by wide-open fields.

    b. A classic New England colonial complete with a white picket fence.

    c. A vintage warehouse with exposed brick and an open-beam ceiling.

    d. A villa that plays homage to the outdoors with a courtyard and a plethora of gardens to explore.

    e. A big city loft with the coolest of Euro kitchens. No fixer-uppers for me.

15. Your ideal sweet treats for wedding day nibbling entail

    a. homemade pies.

    b. a three-tiered vanilla cake with raspberry filling and fondant.

    c. doughnuts and *macarons*.

    d. a cake with buttercream frosting, topped with fresh flowers.

    e. ice-cream sandwiches served from a food truck.

Now tally those answers up, *Teen*-magazine style, and see where you land!

If you have more **A's** . . . you're a chic, rustic bride.

If you have more **B's** . . . you're oh-so-classic.

If you have more **C's** . . . you're whimsically fabulous.

If you have more **D's** . . . al fresco is where it's at.

If you have more **E's** . . . you're all about modern fab.

STEP 3: HIT THE WEB

When it comes to using the Web to guide and direct your wedding style, you might feel like you either won the lottery for all things gorgeous or like you've been smacked in the face with all things totally and completely overwhelming. After all, the most exciting inspiration can be found in the most unexpected of places: a gown round-up from Oscar night, images from favorite travel sites, ideas found on home décor blogs, Web swatches of ribbons and fabrics, prints and patterns you can find through online art galleries. Digital inspiration is a constant, never-ending stream that can easily flip your vision on its head, confusing and frustrating you with every new idea.

Our advice: start with a small handful of sites to help inspire you. There is something for everyone out there, and if you look closely, you'll discover the sites that really resonate with you. Finding the *right* wedding inspiration blog or website and making those a part of your daily routine is key to preserving your sanity.

STEP 4: BUILD INSPIRATION BOARDS

The inspiration board, a tool used to unite all of your must-have ideas and inspirations in one cohesive montage, is perhaps the simplest way to ensure that your vision is translated for each and every vendor that you work with. Using *Style Me Pretty*'s drag-and-drop online board builder, and the gallery of more than 500,000 images, you can play with your board until you find just the right details to articulate your style. If a Web-based interface doesn't fuel your creativity, I've also built boards in Adobe Photoshop and Illustrator, where you can incorporate digital color palettes and text. Or, for the nontechies, simply print out your favorite photographs and ideas and pin them to a bulletin board. Whatever approach you take, crafting an inspiration board (or many) is the best tool that you can use to hone and edit all of the items in your inspiration file system.

STEP 5: DON'T LOOK BACK

When the decisions have been made, when your vision has been decided upon, when you have guided your wedding style to perfection . . . the curse of "buyer's remorse" just might set in. After all, the constant influx of eye candy found simply by turning on your computer can be intoxicating and wildly addicting. But this, my lovelies, is the moment that really counts. This is the moment where you learn to trust yourself and your vision, where you go forth knowing that you are well equipped to not only plan a wedding . . . but to plan one with grace, with substance, and with adoration and respect for all things uniquely you. Print out those inspiration boards and hang them on your wall, keep the swatches of fabric that you carefully selected nearby. And plant a big fat reminder smooch on the one you love. Because it's in that very kiss where you will always find what's most important.

BET YOU DIDN'T THINK you'd get a step-by-step guide tucked into a step-by-step guide! But in order to really grasp the anatomy of a bespoke celebration, you have to first understand the importance in managing your inspiration. It's carefully curating the ideas that you've found along the way that will ultimately give you a great foundation to build your own totally unique wedding. And now that you've mastered that very concept, it's back to the wedding at hand.

 ## SET YOUR COLOR PALETTE

5

Steps 1 to 4 are about finding and keeping the inspiration you've fallen for. It's about setting the groundwork for designing a uniquely-you celebration. And now it's time to layer on the color.

Often, brides and grooms jump straight into selecting their wedding colors—long before they should. In the initial stages of planning, key colors become way too important to some couples. The result means that they are forcing incompatible hues into their favorite venue. Finding the right color palette should be done as carefully and as thoughtfully as any other element within your planning process. The colors do not need to be overly matched or defined, but should rather be a subtle spectrum that brings depth and dimension to your style. They should be derived from your surroundings and married with colors that you and your future hubby love.

SPECIAL TIPS

- **THE BEST WAY TO CREATE** a cohesive and fluid color palette is to allow your space and your style to set the tone. Pull from the backdrop the natural hues that are built into your canvas, and pair those with colors that you love, as well as with contrasting hues to ground the space. A wooden barn, for example, would look gorgeous decked out in swaths of contrasting white fabric, worn wooden accents, and a splash of your favorite color.

- **THE BEST PLACE TO LOOK** to figure out the "colors you love" part of the equation? Just don't forget to look to your other half's side for inspiration, too!

 ## 6 CHOOSE YOUR FLOWERS Choosing the right
Step
flowers can be one of the most overwhelming parts of planning your wedding. We could, in fact, devote an entirely separate book to this element alone. So many different options, so many beautiful colors exist. There are in-season and off-season prices, flowers that cost $5 for a single stem and flowers that cost $5 for an entire bunch. The sheer volume is enough to send any rational bride over the edge. Knowledge is power when it comes to this portion of wedding planning. Whether you work with a great florist or you hit the books yourself, understanding what is available to you in your budget, knowing the textures and colors of flowers that you love, and weeding out what you don't want will all help you to make decisions on floral décor that bring your vision to a new place of lovely.

For Rachael and Justin's wedding, the pair chose hydrangeas, burgundy lady slipper orchids, lots of irises, agapanthus, artichokes, sweet peas, chocolate cosmos, dahlias, ranunculas, lilac, peonies, and roses to execute their vision. The pure refinement of the floral selections set the tone of the entire wedding day décor.

> 66 *We knew that the floral selection was going to be extremely limited based on what the local floral wholesalers were telling us was available. They said they couldn't get anything interesting or special that far into the interior of the country and that remotely because it all died by the time it got to them. Our options were carnations and lilies. FiftyFlowers, an online source, totally saved the day. The wholesale retailer delivered all of the flowers we wanted in the middle of a flood when even major roads were washed out.* 99
> —JOY

SPECIAL TIPS

• **IT'S BEST TO SELECT STEMS** that are seasonally available. It will not only cut the price dramatically but it will also ensure that your blooms don't have to travel too far and that they are fresh and gorgeous on your wedding day.

• **IF YOU'RE HIRING A FLORIST,** choose one who shares your design sensibilities, whose work you resonate with, and who is willing to accommodate your unique budget. Pore over portfolios and galleries until you've found just the right person. Then, using the inspiration boards that you have created, make sure that he or she understands your vision.

• **IF YOU'RE CRAFTING THE FLOWERS** on your own, hit the Web. There are great wholesalers online that can help you achieve the look you want.

7
Step

INFUSE YOUR STYLE WITH WHIMSY

A wedding is a wedding is a wedding... until it gets at least a small dose of whimsy. A little piece of fun will make your guests happy and will leave a long-lasting impression. Even the most luxe affair should have some element of playfulness built into its core—a witty poem read during the ceremony, a meaningful, lighthearted song played during the reception, or hot chocolate chip cookies and ice-cold milk given to guests as the party comes to a close. The smile you bring to their faces is what will prompt the memories and make them gush about your wedding for years and years to come.

SPECIAL TIPS

- **WHIMSY DOESN'T HAVE TO MEAN SILLY.** To me, whimsical weddings capture the spirit of the bride and groom, the little things that make you smile or laugh or kiss spontaneously.

- **FOOD OFFERS WONDERFUL** opportunities to add a splash of whimsy: your grandmother's apple pie recipe tied sweetly onto miniature versions. Petite varieties of your favorite grab-and-go foods . . . burgers and fries, tacos, hot dogs with a shot of baked beans. Have fun with your food and you will find that you have very happy guests.

 Step 8 PERSONALIZE THE DAY Personalize, personalize, personalize. It's the mantra of this book and our blog and the reason that we fell head over heels in love with Rachael and Justin's wedding. Adding your personal style stamp to your wedding day is a concept that can mean many things to many people. For some, it's as simple as rewriting classic vows to reflect those more meaningful to you. For others, it means ditching tried-and-true traditions and coming up with brand-new ones. It means that as you get further into planning the details, you'll want to be sure the results are always significant to you and your one and only. What's the saying? Inspiration is everywhere. Find it, love it, then make it your own.

RACHAEL'S ADVICE TO BRIDES-TO-BE . . . *Try not to forget that it's your wedding and that it needs to be true to who you are as a couple. There are thousands of beautiful weddings and ideas, but at the end of the day, your wedding has to fit you. There definitely were times that we got overwhelmed by all the options, but things came together for us as we kept looking at our inspiration pictures, decided on the aspects that we both loved, and settled on our own personal wedding style.*

66 *We tried to add things to our wedding that were personal and fit us as a couple. We picked songs for the ceremony that were meaningful to us to replace traditional wedding music, and we wrote our own vows. My aunt baked her secret-recipe cookies, a favorite of both of ours, as welcome treats for all our guests, and we wrote personal welcome notes to all our guests letting each person know what he or she means to us. We also designed a wedding map that was filled with meaningful landmarks around the farm and showed nearby family farms, so that our guests could understand the significance of the location.* 99

—RACHAEL

• ONE OF MY FAVORITE WAYS to personalize your wedding is to create a wedding brand. It can be as simple as an icon of something meaningful (a chandelier, a sailboat, a rooster) or something as customized as a monogram. You can thread that brand into so many different wedding elements, from your paper goods to your wedding favors, giving way to a look that is made exclusively for you and the one you love.

Real
Wedding

REAL WEEDINGS

are the *Heart & Soul*

OF *STYLE ME PRETTY*, because seeing covetable weddings is the surest way
to determine what makes your own heart beat faster. Beautiful brides with maids all in a
row, grooms at their finest, cakes and flowers and stationery crafted to utter perfection.
Each and every wedding that we feature on *Style Me Pretty* is chosen for a different reason.
Some are flat-out gorgeous. Others are quirky, or modern, or chic. And others simply make
us smile. Beyond the flawless photography and the moments that make us tear up, though,
there are the details, the wildly unexpected or sweet or beautiful or bursting-with-fun
details that we obsess over every day. To us, it's a really, really great detail that transforms a
nice wedding into an unforgettable one.

So how do you *use* one of those beyond-compare *real weddings* to inspire your own
unique day?

The answer is simple. You break it apart. You take out the pieces and look at each
detail as an individual, as a color or a texture or a moment. A beautiful bouquet, for
example, is also a painter's palette that can help determine your wedding colors. A
gown—in silhouette, in texture, in style—can inspire an exquisite tablescape for your own

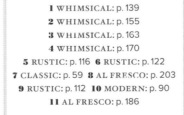

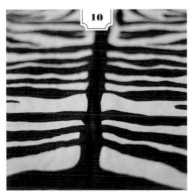

celebration. A venue, despite being nowhere near you, can trigger a pull to a particular type of scenery or ambiance that you might want to incorporate. And hearing the story behind the wedding, as told by the bride and groom, can help put your own day into perspective, reminding you that all of those handcrafted moments spell out who you are as a couple.

Included in this next chapter are sixteen of the most beautiful real weddings I could get my hands on, all falling into five unique style categories: Classic, Modern, Rustic, Whimsical, and Al Fresco. Many of them overlap from one category to the next, marrying homegrown details into classic ballrooms and modern execution into rustic spaces. The styles and details we've chosen were made to be mixed and matched, to be layered, to be reworked and recrafted to suit your own unique vision. Use these weddings as inspirations, as idea launching pads, all with the notion that you can put your style stamp on each and every one, transforming the foundation of the wedding into one that fits you and your soon-to-be like a well-worn glove.

STYLE *Blueprints*

AS AN ADDED BONUS, I've partnered with a dream team of wedding vendors to craft couture blueprints based on each style concept. Every blueprint is filled with ideas that you can find in mainstream stores, both in rentals and in products available for purchase that fit within the scope of a specific wedding style. We wanted our designers, who often craft million-dollar fêtes, to show you that neither your location nor your budget should limit the level of lovely that you can achieve—that weddings as enviable as those in this book are actually just a series of puzzle pieces, thoughtfully and carefully executed, all coming together into a beautiful whole.

WEDDINGS

FOR AS MANY WEDDINGS AS I LOOK AT DAY IN AND
day out, it's always the classically inspired weddings, the weddings with ceremony,
tradition, and timeless style, that bring back the moment when I was five years old,
dreaming about marrying Prince Charming. It's the Audrey in me, the Grace Kelly,
the little girl who danced around in a belted bedsheet marrying one Cabbage Patch doll
after another. You see, I love formalities. I love black-and-white palettes, and ball gowns
and calligraphy. I love Pachelbel's *Canon,* cotton candy flower girls, and *"with this ring, I
thee wed."* I love the classics and I believe in the quiet romance built into tradition. But
what I love most about this first set of real weddings is that *classic* means giving yourself
permission to redefine tradition and infuse your day with your own sense of style and
grace. These celebrations are classic . . . with a twist.

White Wedding
PERFECTION

THIS ULTRACRISP, classically chic wedding had me at hello. Vero Beach is home to some of the prettiest seaside weddings I've seen, but this particular fête takes postcard-perfect to a place of total love. Every last whitewashed touch was effortlessly designed so that each moment, each detail is as lovely on its own as it is as a whole.

From a style perspective, Megan and Greg saw their day as simple, understated, and timeless, with a touch of that preppy island feel that Vero Beach invites. Low, lush white florals, lots and lots of white candles, twisted willow branches, and strands of twinkle lights set the tone for all-out stunning. But more important than aesthetics, this bride and groom wanted their day to be intimate and completely personal. And from where I sit . . . mission accomplished.

BRIDE & GROOM: *Megan & Greg* •
LOCATION: *Vero Beach, FL* • FLOWERS: *white hydrangeas,*
white peonies, garden roses, green viburnum

THE CELEBRATION AND MARRIAGE

Megan Susanne Mollmu

AND

Greg William Sleig

JUNE 18, 2011

WINDSOR CHAPE

VERO BEACH, FLO

Special Touches For each of our guests, I put together welcome baskets with some of our favorite foods: San Pellegrino sparkling water, old-fashioned Diet Cokes, Carr's crackers and cheese, oranges, and dark chocolate. My eldest four nephews served as ushers; my three oldest nieces walked down the aisle with their younger brothers; and our littlest nieces served as our flower girls. It was definitely the kids who stole the show.

> 66 *May you have a happy and successful marriage.*
> *May God bless your marriage and your children.*
> *May we remind you that a good marriage is based on*
>   *friendship as well as love.*
> *When children find true love, their parents find true joy.*
> *To your joy and ours from this day forward!* 99
> —MEGAN'S FATHER'S TRADITIONAL TOAST

Advice Just remember, your wedding probably won't turn out exactly like the one you saw in a magazine. It will be a reflection of all these little choices that you and your fiancé made along the way. And it will be better, because it will be yours.

BRIDE'S JEWELRY: With a lace dress and lace-trimmed veil, Megan kept her jewelry simple. Her "something borrowed" was a pair of diamond earrings borrowed from her mother, and a beaded belt by Monique Lhuillier was added. WEDDING GOWN: Inspired by her sister's lace wedding dress, Megan opted for a gown that was sweet and romantic.

Reserved

GROOM'S ATTIRE WATCH: The watch was a groom's gift from the bride, now known affectionately as the nicest thing anyone has ever bought him. Greg chose his navy suit from Ermenegildo Zegna with a tie from John Varvatos. Ushers and ring bearers wore blue gingham shirts from J. Crew and Sperry topsiders. CENTERPIECES: To create an intimate, inviting space, classic low floral arrangements filled with white roses, peonies, and hydrangeas served as centerpieces.

Understated
& INSPIRED

THIS WEDDING is a lesson in editing. Sometimes crafting a classic wedding means working with a muted palette that allows the details to really sparkle. The bride and groom conceptualized a design that was simultaneously quiet and chic, so the delicious details stood out against their simple canvas. The result? Total wedding magic. From the ruffled cake to the lace table runner, every last touch was kissed by pretty.

BRIDE & GROOM: *Misherr & Benjamin* • LOCATION: *Los Angeles, CA* •
FLOWERS: *white and blush peonies, anemones, white scabiosa, white ranunculus, white astilbe, dusty miller, flowering oregano, stock, seeded eucalyptus*

MR. & MRS. FRANK TSENG AND JENNIFER YI WITH
MR. & MRS. DAVID AND MARIA WONG
REQUEST THE PLEASURE OF YOUR COMPANY
AT THE MARRIAGE OF THEIR CHILDREN

MISHERR TSENG
TO
BENJAMIN WONG

6.18.2011
LOS ANGELES, CALIFORNIA

THREE O'CLOCK IN THE AFTERNOON AT
SAINT TIMOTHY CATHOLIC CHURCH
10425 WEST PICO BOULEVARD

COCKTAIL AND DINNER RECEPTION TO FOLLOW AT
SMOGSHOPPE
2651 SOUTH LA CIENEGA BOULEVARD

Special Touches
As a self-proclaimed dog lady, I made sure to include some fun dog elements in the details. For example, instead of numerals, we used different dog-breed silhouettes as table numbers. We also incorporated silhouettes of our two dogs on our wedding paper goods, such as programs and menus. And instead of favors, we decided to donate to the ASPCA. • We also made sure our guests' stomachs were happy by incorporating fun foods like mini-sliders for appetizers, mini-ice cream cones, and a late-night taco stand.

GUEST BOOKS: The note card guest books, designed by Martha Stewart, allowed space for Misherr and Benjamin to insert their wedding brand, the puppy silhouette, and to create cohesion among all of their paper pieces.

the pomeranian

DOG SILHOUETTES: Coming from a huge family of dog lovers, the bride and groom incorporated breeds that they know and love. Misherr intentionally used mixed breeds to celebrate the awesomeness of all dogs. DESSERT TABLE: Misherr and Benjamin, who both have a huge sweet tooth, chose their favorite desserts to grace the table. From mini-cupcakes and crème brûlée to the pink ruffled cake that the bride obsessed over, every little bit of the spread was so "them."

Organic ELEGANCE

THIS WEDDING IS PROOF that simplicity and style make for the perfect combination. The bride and groom wanted a fête that was classic yet organic, effortless yet timeless. They infused so much of their personality into their day that the flawless design served only as a canvas for the layers upon layers of total, unabashed charm.

Jaclyn and Brandon chose a venue rich in history and stunning tradition, built in the 1800s on more than 300 acres of land.

BRIDE & GROOM: *Jaclyn & Brandon* •
LOCATION: *Lenox, MA* • FLOWERS: *spray roses, Juliet garden roses, white peonies, white stock, white veronica*

Special Touches

The most important elements were those that made the day feel like it was our wedding and not just any wedding! For the ceremony, the top of the chuppah was made of three very special fabrics: (1) fabric from my wedding dress, (2) fabric from the hat my mom got married in, and (3) fabric from the hat that Brandon's mom got married in. Plus, our rabbi married my parents over thirty years ago!

WOODEN ESCORT CARDS: The escort cards were handcrafted by the bride and her mother using freshly cut birch discs they found on Etsy. **CHUPPAH:** A local Massachusetts designer, Cassandra Holden, crafted the stunning chuppah, which the couple's event designer gussied up using birch-tree posts and understated florals.

Advice When it comes to your wedding day, spend time talking to your vendors and your significant other and listen to your own instincts as to what you really want.

• We didn't take ourselves too seriously. After we kissed and the ceremony was complete, our recessional song was "I'm a Believer" by the Monkees. We love the first few lines and the upbeat sound, but we secretly chose it because it reminded us of *Shrek*!

TREES: Inspired by the Berkshires landscape where they became engaged, Jaclyn and Brandon wanted to honor the beauty of the outdoors in their reception space. Two trees flanked either side of the room, creating a whimsical but nature-inspired environment. **CAMEO BROOCH:** The cameo was a wonderful way to celebrate the bride's great-grandmother, lovingly called Fuffa.

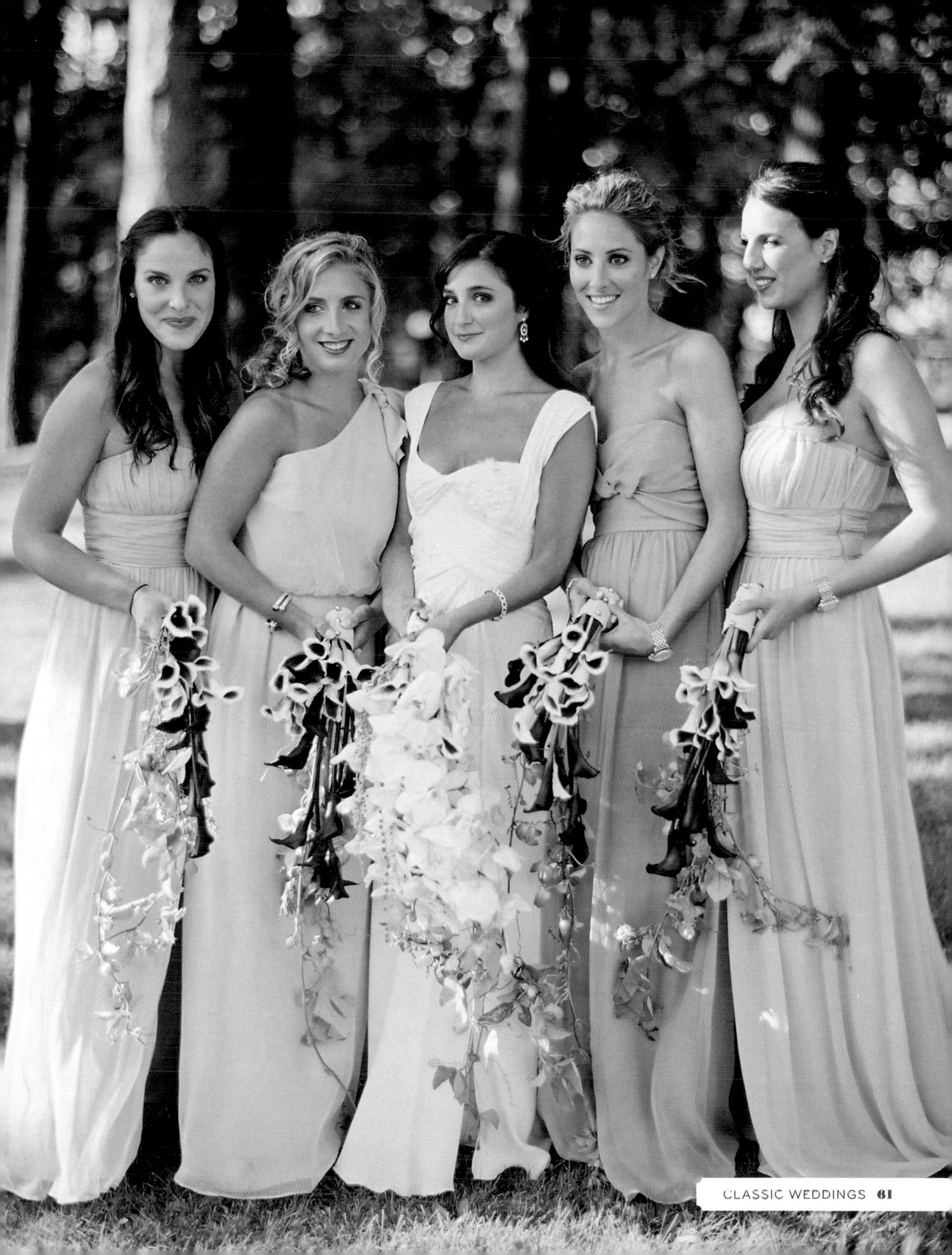

KIPPOT: The couple chose the Star of David to adorn the men's kippot made by a small community of Jews in Uganda. Through the charity Kippot for Hope, 100 percent of proceeds for the pieces support underprivileged Jewish communities in Uganda—thus the couple felt that they were incorporating a bit of mitzvah (a good deed) into their first day of marriage. **LAVENDER CONES (previous spread):** The lavender tucked inside the cones was meant to be tossed as the bride and groom walked down the aisle during their recessional, though the guests didn't get the memo—proof that even the best-laid plans are often foiled! Despite the folly, the bundles added an aura of beauty throughout the mansion and the reception.

Blueprint

NO 1

CLASSIC

THERE IS SOMETHING SO INNATELY LUXURIOUS

about tradition and formality. And when it comes to weddings, it's the classics that stand the test of time. We found that crafting a classic wedding blueprint was as inspiring as watching an old Bogart movie, and we allowed that love of tradition to guide the way. Start by spending time learning the bones of wedding etiquette, about the importance of editing so that only the most luxurious and lovely details shine through, and that simple is often the most beautiful approach. Then vow to yourself that you will infuse your own classic wedding with personality and that special something that makes you and your fiancé unique.

COLOR PALETTE

1

WHEN SETTING YOUR TABLE, look to the classics. The Post girls can be your guide, ensuring you provide a flawless collection of cutlery, stemware, and presentation to knock the socks off each and every one of your guests. Layering classic china patterns with heirloom silver or adorning each place setting with a hand-calligraphed menu is a perfect way to set the tone.

· TABLESCAPE ·

2

USING ANTIQUE INSPIRED TEXTILES like lace will bring In a sense of tradition without overpowering the design.

3

ADD A SPECIAL SOMETHING to each place setting to let guests know that they are dining with taste: a saltcellar, a classic place-card holder, any simple but pretty detail that can elevate the whole experience. Silver serving trays are a timeless detail that will totally raise the style count on your traditional tablescape. Used to ground the design and provide weight to your palette, a collection of found vintage trays is an apropos accessory.

4

IF YOUR BUDGET IS TIGHT, consider making a single head table the focal point for the evening. Deck it out with over-the-top lace chair covers, stunning linens, chic monochromatic flowers, fruitwood Chiavari chairs— an overall feeling of total luxury. Keep it simple on the neighboring tables with white linens (or our DIY doily overlay featured among our projects; see page 220) and a single bouquet of baby's breath.

5

A HANDWRITTEN MENU topping each place setting offers a moment of pure indulgence, giving your guests a glimpse of what's to come.

6

DINING BY CANDLELIGHT is a quintessential classic technique. Mix and match tall taper candles in pretty candleholders (we've seen them everywhere, from area flea markets to local craft stores) with mercury-glass votives and silver details.

1 NOTHING SAYS CLASSIC
like a sea of white stems.

· FLORALS ·

2 APPEASE THE SENSES
with an arrangement that is not only
easy on the eyes but also full of
delicious fragrance and soft textures.
Paired with candlelight in crystal bowls, the effect
is warm and luxurious.

3 TUCK SINGLE BLOOMS into
crystal vessels around larger arrangements
to create an interesting and elegant display
with a medley of heights and sizes.

4 MIX AND MATCH expensive florals—
dare we say, peonies—with wispy, white stems
in bulk, like baby's breath or Queen Anne's
lace. Tucked beautifully into a cut-crystal vase, the result is a
seamless balance of tradition and style—without breaking the
budget.

CENTERPIECE FLOWERS: mint, Queen Anne's lace, dahlias, hellebores, snowberries, astilbe, hyacinths, and French anemones · **BOUQUET FLOWERS:** snowberries, ranunculus, French anemones, and hyacinths

· CAKE ·

1 WHEN DESIGNING your classic cake, think about sweet ways you can capture the style of your day without being boring. As an example, the black detailing on this cake adds a hint of modern sensibility.

2 LET YOUR WEDDING GOWN inspire the cake. In this case, ruffles and fabric detailing were inspired by a black-and-white gown that our cake designer spotted online.

3 PRESENTATION IS EVERYTHING. For this cake, the designer opted for a traditional pedestal cake stand updated with a lacquerlike, contemporary-feeling finish.

1 CLASSIC BLACK CALLIGRAPHY

will set the tone for your rooted-in-tradition wedding. This set has been updated with white calligraphy on black paper and whimsical silhouettes representing various moments throughout the wedding weekend.

2 USING A CLASSIC

wedding font available in a store may make the pieces feel too stale or expected. Reinvent your paper pieces by bringing in a calligrapher who will custom write your invitation.

· PAPER GOODS ·

4 FOR THE LINER, we chose

an elegant pattern inspired by King Louis XIV's court. It almost looks like strokes from a fountain pen. Classic dark inks—black, deep purple, navy, charcoal, or the darkest of dark browns—pulled together the whole suite.

5 EVEN IF YOU AREN'T

working with a designer, remember the mantra: keep it simple and decidedly elegant. When in doubt, ask, "What would Princess Grace do?"

3 IMPERIAL-SIZED CARDS

are larger than the standard rectangle, so they feel a bit more regal and grand.

Modern WEDDINGS

MODERN WEDDINGS, HOW I HEART YOU SO. It's the simplicity in style, the understated chic, and the mad love peeking out of every effortless detail. It's the clean lines, the edited approach, the fabulous color palettes that allow for the celebration and ceremony to really shine. My heart skips a beat every time I see a modern fête done so very right, and in this next chapter, we've found three of the most spectacular.

ROOFTOP GARDEN
Chic

WE DON'T SEE NEARLY ENOUGH ROOFTOP WEDDINGS. The setting sun, the take-your-breath-away views, the chic, modern styling. A rooftop wedding is the recipe for swoon central and it's the backdrop for this next pretty little number. It was love at first sight for me with this Hollywood bash, and the gorgeous bride and groom who are so crazy about each other just made it that much more addicting.

Timeless, classic, and decidedly chic was the vision that Gina and Justin had for their wedding. Designing a day that elevated the beauty of their venue was important to the pair, as was crafting an evening where their guests could kick back and really enjoy themselves, just as they would if they were attending a wedding in the couple's own backyard. Simple green and white peonies, freesia, and orchids graced white linens; twinkle lights were strung from one side of the dance floor to the other; and Chinese lanterns gave the entire reception an added glow. The recipe was set for an evening of unabashed celebration.

BRIDE & GROOM: *Gina & Justin* • LOCATION: *Hollywood, CA* •
FLOWERS: *green lady slipper orchids, white Phalaenopsis orchids, succulents, green Cymbidium orchids, white freesia, green and white peonies*

Special Touches

Aside from our ceremony, the single most important part of our day was the party. The food from the Gordon Ramsay restaurant was amazing, and the red velvet cake made by SusieCakes was the perfect sweet treat to finish the meal.

• I'm not a big DIY type of bride, but I did think it was important to have a few elements that were undoubtedly unique. I hand made my sash with a few different shades of silk organza and some good old-fashioned love! Also, the wedding favors—which were meant to be a little take-home, late-night version of our wedding cake—were boxed and wrapped with help from my family the night before the wedding

SHOES: Found at Barneys in Beverly Hills, the bride's shoes were chosen knowing that they would look equally fabulous with a great pair of jeans as they would a formal wedding gown. **BOUQUET:** Romantic and decidedly girly were the only rules for the bride's bouquet. And peonies fit the bill to perfection.

Advice

If I could give brides any advice, I would tell them three things: (1) Hire a wedding planner. Mine was just perfect and kept me as relaxed as I could possibly be on the day of the wedding. She was my voice, my brain, and my common sense on a day when I lacked all three of these! (2) Find a superamazing photographer to capture all the right moments since you may succumb to what I called my "wedding amnesia." (3) Enjoy the day—the vows, the kiss, the dance, the love between each other, and the love from your friends and family supporting you in your special moment.

SUCCULENTS: Living in Los Angeles, the bride developed a love for succulents. She chose them for her wedding day décor to capture the natural, organic vibe of a rooftop garden. **SIGNATURE COCKTAIL:** Concocted by a good friend of the couple, this Grapefruit on the Rocks cocktail featured pink grapefruit juice, grapefruit vodka, St. Germain Liquor, Domaine de Canton, and lychee juice. **CHESS PIECES** (previous spread): The littlest guests had a blast playing with this whimsical detail of the London Hotel.

1020

North San Vicente Boulevard

THE

LONDON

WEST HOLLYWOOD

OX
OD
C   F E
BY GO   N RAMSAY

GORDON RAMSAY
AT THE LONDON

VENUE: The London Hotel held special meaning for the couple. Having dined there many times before the wedding, they always loved the feel and ambience of the space. It is boutique inspired and yet quietly understated—the perfect backdrop for their wedding. By adding a few flowers and simple lights, the canvas sparkled all on its own. **CAKE:** The cake was a decadent red velvet cake covered in cream-cheese icing. The green orchids gave a little pop of color to an otherwise simple and handmade style.

MODERN *Vintage*

THIS NEXT WEDDING IS A COMBINATION OF EVERYTHING wonderful found in a bespoke celebration. It's filled to the brim with style, the details are off-the-charts pretty, the modern approach is both whimsical and yet firmly rooted in tradition. But the thing that I love most is that each and every detail is meaningful, overflowing with honest, authentic personality. The result is total wedding fabulousness.

The inspiration for Carly and Robert's wedding was soulful and rich and embraced the 1950s and '60s spirit that defines the couple's personal aesthetic. Sofia Coppola's commercial film for Christian Dior's fragrance Miss Dior, plus the cult classic *The Red Balloon* (*Le Ballon Rouge*), a French film from the 1950s, served as the inspiration for the wedding. Held at The Chambers Hotel, an art hotel owned by the famed Walker Art Center's biggest donor, Ralph Burnett, the pair selected round tables with handcrafted menus on each place setting, stunning floral arrangements inspired by Marie Antoinette with pale pink and coral miniature roses, and an innate sense of vintage style to permeate every last detail of the day.

BRIDE & GROOM: *Carly & Robert* •
LOCATION: *Minneapolis, MN* • FLOWERS: *black magic roses, pink esperance roses, green and pink hydrangeas*

84

LOVE
LOUDER
THAN
THUNDER

SPECIAL THANKS
Cynthia Brown
Nancy Dockter
Scott Meehan
Patricia Oertel
Robert & Gloria Raimondi
Louis Venticinque
Lachlan & Chika Willis

WISH YOU WERE

Harry & Inez Gilso

Special Touches

The fabric for my dress came from the LVMH and Oscar de la Renta mill in Italy and was a 1950s silk gabardine. All the dresses, including the bridesmaids', were custom designed by Avion Feminin. I wanted dresses that embraced the fashion in films like *La Dolce Vita* and paintings by John Singer Sargent in the 1800s. Our groomsmen wore slim, vintage-inspired black suits and they all wore different-colored socks to reflect inspiration from Quentin Tarantino's *Reservoir Dogs,* one of my husband's favorite films. • My husband's family is Italian, so we embraced that concept for our menu. The food was catered by D'Amico, one of the best Italian restaurants in Minneapolis. Our wedding menus were even written in Italian! We served Italian Ice Tea—a recipe made famous at Vincent's in Little Italy back in the '50s.

Advice Enjoy every possible moment, from planning to getting ready to walking down the aisle. It's over before you can blink—seriously! No matter how hard you try to have the perfect wedding, there are going to be minor inconveniences. My mantra was, "Just go with it!"

MUSTACHES: Robert and Carly wanted their wedding photographs to exude untraditional, whimsical joy. Since the style was inspired by *The Red Balloon*/*Miss Dior*/*La Dolce Vita*, the mustache seemed quite fitting.

CENTERPIECES: The bride wanted to capture the spirit of the 1950s with these centerpieces, inspired by *macarons* and *croquembouche* cakes.

Sophisticated LUXURY

I'M A SUCKER FOR A STUNNING ANIMAL PRINT WOVEN INTO wedding design. It's something that I rarely see, and if done well, it can be insanely chic. That's why I must admit—the zebra detailing that was infused into this next wedding instantly gave me a serious case of the wedding jellies—all-out jealousy for what might be one of the most awesome weddings I've ever seen.

Ginny and Mark envisioned their day to be modern and fresh with a focus on glamour—old Hollywood with a twist. They wanted their guests to be able to step back in time for a soulful and yet comfortable evening filled to the brim with luxury. A rich chocolate brown and turquoise palette set the tone for the event. Mercury glass was used in abundance, while stark white florals crafted mostly from orchids graced every last corner. Zebra elements were threaded into the design tastefully through rugs and accessories, even a stenciled print on the dance floor.

BRIDE & GROOM: *Ginny & Mark* • LOCATION: *West Hollywood, CA* • FLOWERS: *white Phalaenopsis orchids, white gardenias, white hydrangeas*

Special Touches We had a custom mercury-glass chuppah made that was such a statement piece and really stole the design show (next spread). In lieu of a traditional rice toss, we had our guests throw mini-streamers during our recessional. It was a fun, festive alternative. • We wanted our guests to be comfortable, so chocolate brown flip-flops were handed out before the dancing began.

Advice Trust your instincts and be true to yourself. You can borrow ideas from different sources and combine them to create your perfect vision.

for after the "I Do's!"

COLOR PALETTE: The couple chose a palette of crisp white, chocolate brown, and a punch of teal. **RECEPTION DÉCOR:** Ginny and Mark loved the idea of combining the modern white suede chairs and white banquettes with the gorgeous custom teal dupioni linens. Adding the mercury glass to this color palette gave it the perfect balance of bling and elegance. **FLOWERS:** The pair made a big floral statement using just one floral type—all-white Phalaenopsis orchids. Pairing them with the mercury-glass vessels gave a clean and classic look with a hint of modern.

Blueprint

NO **2**

MODERN

MODERN MEANS "MINIMAL" in my book. Clean lines, simple color palettes (whether bold or demure), repetition in pattern and style. Although it's a style that is often reserved for blank-canvas lofts and stark art galleries, the edited approach to detailing is something that can work within the context of any wedding style. A can't-look-away gorgeous wedding frequently has modern sensibilities inspired by a single detail or element. So when designing the Modern Blueprint, our designer looked to one of her favorite florals, the succulent, to inspire the design elements. From the square chargers to the slim cutlery, every detail was reserved and yet decidedly chic.

COLOR PALETTE

1 **START WITH AN INSPIRATION POINT.** We loved the idea of building all elements around our succulent table runner.

2 **USE CLEAN LINES** with an emphasis on geometric shapes to play up your modern theme. We opted for white square chargers, accenting them with simple cutlery and casual barware. This kept the vibe contemporary and yet approachable.

· TABLESCAPE ·

3 **ALLOW YOUR DESIGN** to get a little bit playful. Fun metal straws were used to add a bit of conversation and whimsy to the table.

4 **THINK OUTSIDE THE BOX** a bit when looking for inspiration. Pulling ideas from some of her favorite restaurants, our designer opted for an antique farm table for an effect that felt a bit more like home.

5 PLAY WITH DIFFERENT
SEATING OPTIONS. A gently worn
bench becomes modern when accessorized
so simply. You could throw some cushions on it to invite
your guests to get comfortable and stay a while.

6 REPEAT, REPEAT, REPEAT.
Repetition is key in creating a cohesive modern design. Our color palette, our prints, and the placement of décor elements on the table were all in perfectly repetitive harmony.

1 **WHEN IT COMES** to contemporary florals, simplicity is the key. Keep flowers monochromatic in hue and use repetition to create that wow factor. Our event and floral designers envisioned a succulent table runner that screamed chic, totally sustainable style.

· FLORALS ·

2 **SMALL VOTIVES** add a bit of romance to the look and soften it so that guests feel that casual vibe that you've built in with your other elements.

3 **BRING IN A BIT OF WARMTH.** We used peachy hues tucked into the bridal bouquet to do just that. The softness of the stems adds to the casual, effortlessly organic nature of this modern style.

CENTERPIECE FLOWERS: succulent table runner
BOUQUET FLOWERS: Oncidium and Phalaenopsis orchids, succulents

1 LET THE CAKE TAKE CENTER STAGE.

Our designer used the same clean lines and detailing found in our tablescape to craft the cake. This two-tiered version of a wedding cake is a fresher approach to an otherwise traditional design. Accented with sugar succulents, the look is fabulously modern while still rooted in tradition.

· CAKE ·

2 TO BRING IN THAT SAME SENSE OF HOME,

our designer adorned the cake table with antique cutlery and silver-hued plates. The cake is placed on a vintage platter to soften the lines and capture a feeling of home.

· PAPER GOODS ·

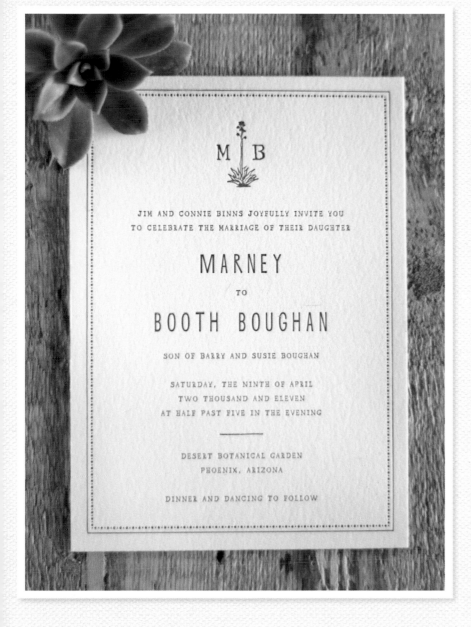

JIM AND CONNIE BINNS JOYFULLY INVITE YOU
TO CELEBRATE THE MARRIAGE OF THEIR DAUGHTER

MARNEY

TO

BOOTH BOUGHAN

SON OF BARRY AND SUSIE BOUGHAN

SATURDAY, THE NINTH OF APRIL
TWO THOUSAND AND ELEVEN
AT HALF PAST FIVE IN THE EVENING

———

DESERT BOTANICAL GARDEN
PHOENIX, ARIZONA

DINNER AND DANCING TO FOLLOW

 WHEN IT COMES TO MODERN
invitations, simplicity is key in color and in style. In this case, we stuck to a single hue: kelly green. By pairing it with stark white paper, our color and design really popped.

2 **MODERN DOESN'T MEAN COLD.**
We added warmth and whimsy to our invitations by introducing a series of inspired icons—a cowboy boot, a silhouette, a boat, and a beach umbrella—each signifying a portion of the wedding weekend.

 WE CAREFULLY SELECTED
two modern-with-a-hint-of-tradition typefaces and skipped using any script fonts. The larger sans serif font set the contemporary tone for the entire invitation suite.

Rustic WEDDINGS

SWEET, SIMPLY STYLED RUSTIC WEDDINGS are in large part what helped put wedding blogs on the map. But it's the rustic weddings, *really done right,* that get the giddies going. That means gorgeous, elegant details paired with the creature comforts of homegrown affairs. Freshly baked pies sitting underneath chandeliers, plaid napkins tied with gold twine resting on fine china . . . It's hard not to love the layered, handcrafted nature of a rustic wedding, the family spirit that seems to be woven into every last detail. The weddings that follow represent a fresh, timeless spin on this otherwise homespun style. Think calligraphy as a nod to the classics, tiered handmade wedding cakes, snipped-from-the-garden flowers tied with the most gorgeous raw silk ribbon. It's rustic . . . elevated.

Effortless GRACE

OH IKAT, HOW DO I LOVE THEE? If ever there was a bash that captured the sentiments of a Rustic Chic wedding to perfection . . . it would be this one. With the wish-it-was-mine fabric, the shockingly beautiful handmade details, and the sense of lovely that just demands attention, it's a wedding that could very well serve as the tipping point to entice you to host your own rustic celebration. It's also one that will most certainly redefine what it means to be rustic fabulous.

BRIDE & GROOM: *Patricia & Charles* • LOCATION: *Jackson Hole, WY* • FLOWERS: *Queen Anne's lace, joe-pye weed, peach Juliet garden roses, Darcy garden roses, Miranda garden roses, antique pink/green hydrangeas, pink peonies, green lemon leaf wreaths, pink astilbe, dahlias*

Special Touches

Charles and I lived in Jackson Hole for five years after college and one of the things we cherished most was a moose we fondly named Harriet. She lived near Charles's cabin and we loved Harriet like a family loves their dog. From this, our stationer designed our wedding logo—a bull moose looking at a cow moose with a pink heart in between—that was used in the Save the Dates as well as throughout the rest of the paper pieces.

Advice

Start early making notes of your likes and dislikes. Then hire your wedding planner/coordinator! Make sure it is someone you are comfortable with personally as well as professionally. You will be spending a lot of time with her/him.

GROOM'S CAKE: The groom's cake was crafted in celebration of the groom's love of the Washington Redskins. **HAND-CUT TREE CHARGERS:** The chargers were hand cut from birch trees found on the designer's land a month before the wedding. **IKAT LINENS:** After searching for the right shade of blue, the designer found the Ikat fabric and worked with a local seamstress to custom make all of the accent linens. From the cake table to the bar linens, the pillows and even the pole drapes, each piece was made bespoke for the pair's celebration.

THE CELEBRATION AND BLESSING
OF THE MARRIAGE OF

Patricia Barlow Smith

and

Charles Alexander Kempe

SATURDAY, THE SIXTEENTH OF JULY
TWO THOUSAND AND ELEVEN

SAINT JOHN'S EPISCOPAL CHURCH
JACKSON HOLE, WYOMING

SWEET

Rustic Romance

WHEN RUSTIC WEDDINGS TAKE ON A CHIC, refined design approach, it's the perfect marriage of form and function. This wedding has captured that sentiment to utter perfection. Emily and Anand hosted a summer evening filled with close friends and family, and with unexpected touches around every corner. From the visually stunning chalkboard art, now holding its own as home décor, to the vintage dessert plates, every last detail was thoughtfully crafted and beautifully executed.

BRIDE & GROOM: *Emily & Anand* • LOCATION: *Montevallo, AL* • FLOWERS: *white garden roses, spray roses, fresh blueberries, green viburnum, white hydrangeas*

EAT, Drink and BE MARRIED.

EMILY and ANAND

Special Touches

We hosted the wedding at The American Village, a venue modeled after colonial America, which had green pastures and gardens for guests to stroll. • The barn gave the reception its southern and rustic charm accented by clean white linens, lighting strung from rafters, sweet tea–filled mason jars, live bluegrass music, and whimsical antlers hanging over a dessert table with blueberry-adorned espresso chocolate cake. • Each of our table arrangements, filled with cream hydrangeas, pale pink roses, hypericum berries, and dusty, silver foliage, was designed as if handpicked from a garden.

Advice Start by building an image database of style elements from blogs and your favorite real weddings that best encapsulate your vision. Then sift through those images and find a precious few that stand out, from which you can begin to build a portfolio of ideas.

CHALKBOARD ART: The chalkboard art idea was actually born from a rather unsightly problem. The walls of the reception space, a barn which is normally the starting point for tours of the property, housed large billboards with information about the area. To cover the eyesore, the couple chose to hang large chalkboards that would both serve as added décor and capture the spirit of the day. **BLUEBERRY JAM FAVORS:** Emily wanted a southern-inspired wedding with vintage details. The favors were crafted to roll charm plus homegrown goodness into one adorable gift.

We

EMILY JACKSON
and
ANAND IYER

together with our families, invite you to share in

Our Wedding Day

SUNDAY | 05-08-11 | 6:30 PM

The American Village Chapel · Montevallo, Alabama

Emily and Anand IYER · 5.8.2011 · They Do

CHALKBOARD GUEST BOOK: In lieu of a traditional guest book, the chalkboard variation was a whimsical approach. A vintage typewriter held a letter to guests encouraging them to sign the board. BANNERS: The handmade banners were given to the guests to wave as Emily and Anand exited the barn.

Summer Camp
CHARM

WE ALL REMEMBER THE QUAINT deliciousness of summer camp. But guess what happens when you saturate that homespun style with a sense of elegance and whimsy? Well, you get this little piece of wedding heaven, complete with the prettiest robin's-egg blue Chiavari chairs a girl could ever wish for, a big ol' canoe used to chill refreshments, and the most adorable bride and groom ever.

It might be hard to imagine transforming a bare-bones mess hall into pure magic, but that is precisely what Kelly and Mark did. Kelly wanted a camplike theme, so medals and awards became a common thread through their paper goods, table numbers, escort cards, and décor elements. Vintage tins and silver teapots were used on the tables, and blue mason jars were brought in for color. In the end, the quaint campsite was converted into something wedding dreams are made of.

BRIDE & GROOM: *Kelly & Mark* • LOCATION: *Annapolis, MD*
• FLOWERS: *yellow finesse roses, yellow ranunculus, dusty miller, silver brunia berries, yellow Craspedia*

Special Touches
My favorite memory of the day was walking into the ceremony and watching the look on Mark's face when he saw me for the first time. I fought back tears and was overwhelmed at the sight of our beautiful room—packed with friends and family.

Advice There is so much that is completely out of your control on your wedding day. Our wedding day certainly had the potential for some stressful situations, but I was completely relaxed and enjoyed every minute because I had faith in the professionals I had chosen.

ROBIN'S-EGG BLUE CHIAVARI CHAIRS: The blue chairs were one of the bride's must-haves from the very beginning. **FAVORS:** S'mores fit the camp-inspired bill. The couple's stationer printed the wedding logo on muslin bags, then the pair filled them with all the fixin's—graham crackers, chocolate, and marshmallows. **SEATING CARD DISPLAY (next spread):** Taking inspiration from the camp's award and trophy hall, the escort-card board was crafted to mimic an award plaque, with the cards themselves as award plates. Kelly coordinated with the woodshop teacher and his students at the middle school where she works to have them craft the plaque and the bases exclusively for her wedding.

CANOE: The canoe was borrowed from the camp and served as the perfect beverage holder. **SIGNATURE COCKTAIL:** A spiked lemonade with fresh mint evoked endless summer days . . . all grown up. **PIE BAR:** Rather than having a traditional cake display, the couple hoped to capture a "camp commissary" spin on the trendy dessert bar concept.

Blueprint NO 3

RUSTIC

RUSTIC IS ROMANTIC. Rustic is feminine. Rustic weddings can be so incredibly beautiful, a perfect combination of all that is good in wedding design, that we often find ourselves staring with huge smiles as we unveil every last lovely detail. But the weddings that really give us the wedding chills are those that approach this now-iconic style with a sense of quiet luxury and grace. Bringing in somewhat opulent details, like beautiful silver or high-end china, to an otherwise homespun style—that's what captures our hearts each and every time. That's exactly how we approached this next blueprint: rustic with an effortless glam factor thrown in.

COLOR PALETTE

1 **START WITH TEXTURE.** A burlap runner placed lovingly across our antique farm table adds texture and dimension to our design. This is organic elegance at its finest.

2 **A FARM TABLE** adorned with antique benches is the perfect canvas for a rustic, elegant affair. The richness of the wood reminds guests of dining with friends, of sharing a meal in their home. If renting a series of farm tables isn't in the budget, go all out with your head table and then adorn neighboring tables with a burlap or linen table covering.

3 **STICK WITH A COLOR PALETTE** of warm, inviting neutrals. We love the idea of pretty, feminine peach hues accenting a simple cream-and-brown palette. The peach added that hint of girly gorgeousness to our otherwise understated palette.

to add big texture: votives wrapped in rope, wine bottles wrapped in burlap, menus wrapped in twine. This organic texture will go a long way in creating a look and feel that is layered.

5 BRING IN SOME METALLIC HUES to give your aesthetic a sense of glamour. Gold mixed with rustic textures like twine, burlap, and wood can set the tone for the entire evening. Think gold-rimmed serveware, vintage gold vases used to house florals, gold stemware and cutlery.

6 INEXPENSIVE TABLE WINE, wrapped in burlap sleeves, can serve double duty. It will add to the home-inspired décor and will give your guests something to do: make sure every glass is always filled.

7 THE SMALLEST OF DETAILS count in a rustic affair. Tuck a sprig of olive leaves into each guest's napkin for a pretty, elegant look.

1 THINK DELICIOUS when it comes to your centerpiece. Peaches are both beautiful and totally relevant to our homespun, rustic style. Accent with small juice cups filled with big blossoms and you have a total (budget-pleasing) show stealer.

2 ON THIS TABLE, lush garden roses and lilies in pretty peach and coral hues look like they were picked from the garden at their peak. Pairing the more expensive stems, like garden roses, with a less expensive but equally pretty filler, like stock, will be easier on the budget.

CENTERPIECE FLOWERS: bowls of peaches, garden roses,
olive greens, peach stock · **BOUQUET FLOWERS:** garden roses,
amaryllis, peach stock, dahlias, and olive greens

1 FOR A SOFT, romantic look, opt for an ivory-based cake rather than white.

2 THINK ABOUT USING SOFT LINES when it comes to the structure of your cake. This scallop-edged cake is both traditional and yet decidedly romantic.

3 INSPIRED BY THE FLORALS from the tablescape, this cake was adorned with lush sugar flowers in a dramatic cluster.

1 INCORPORATE HANDMADE DRAWINGS

In your design to infuse a sense of "personal." In this suite, our stationer sketched the bride's avocado farm. The tree on the reply card is an avocado tree from the couple's backyard.

2 USE TWO COMPLEMENTARY FONTS

to add a sense of interest to your paper goods. Mixing a hand-drawn script with a serif font creates harmony on the page.

3 KEEP THE COLOR PALETTE CONSISTENT.

The stationer selected the same muted colors based in nature that our designer used. Corals, rose pinks, and golds set the tone for our invitation suite.

4 LAYERING IN NATURAL ELEMENTS

like twine and kraft paper gives each piece depth and ties back into the table concept that our designer crafted.

Whimsical
WEDDINGS

OFFICIALLY MY NEW FAVORITE BREED OF WEDDING
IS THE WHIMSICAL WEDDING. The only rule is that there aren't
any rules. Ribbon chandeliers, circus-inspired details, balloons, prints and patterns,
total unabashed fun. It's the kind of wedding that leaves guests smiling the whole way
home, that leaves us talking and laughing for years to come. And this set of whimsical
celebrations has absolutely swoontastic details and a sense of cool that is built into the
very structure of the day. Although the elements behind these darling fêtes will leave
you speechless . . . it's the pure, crazy love that will always steal the show.

Handcrafted GOODNESS

THIS JUST MIGHT BE the most fabulously crafted, whimsical wedding I've ever seen. The bride and her family made every last detail—down to the showstopper of a chandelier.

Tristen and Katherine knew that they wanted a classic wedding rewritten with spunk, more akin to a cocktail party than a formal reception. They said their vows before their immediate families, bridal party, and Katherine's grandfather, then hosted an intimate gathering for eighty-five. Using inspiration found from an eclectic list, including their favorite film, *Amélie,* their shared love of literature, vintage Chicago postcards, the 1930s Chicago World's Fair, and Anthropologie's ethereal window displays, Tristen and Katherine just might be the proud recipients of the world's most smile-inducing celebration.

BRIDE & GROOM: *Katherine & Tristen* • LOCATION: *Chicago, IL* • FLOWERS: *coral charm peonies, yellow Craspedia, peach mini Calla lilies, peach garden roses, white Veronica*

Katherine Sontag
& Tristen Shields

June 4th, 2011

A NEW LEAF • CHICAGO, IL

Special Touches

I always envisioned creating some kind of fabric installation for the reception, and the high ceiling in our reception space lent the perfect opportunity. We came up with the idea of constructing a two-tiered fabric chandelier to add color, texture, and warmth to the modern space. My father built the frame, then both of my parents generously hand cut each and every yard of fabric—a project that lovingly became known as *The Beast*. • Two swing jazz guitarists performed during the ceremony, and Tristen had me wait until I walked down the aisle to hear the song he had chosen for my entrance, which was "Pure Imagination" from *Willy Wonka & the Chocolate Factory*.

RSVP

KINDLY REPLY BY MAY 3, 2011

M _____

○ Will be there with bells on!
○ Will be there without bells.
○ Will be there...undecided on bells.
○ Will not be there...heard there
   might be people wearing bells.
○ Will not be there...regardless of
   the bell debate.

MR. & MRS. DAVID SONTAG
1528 West Schubert Avenue
Chicago, Illinois
6-0-6-1-4

TOGETHER WITH THEIR FAMILIES

TRISTEN
and
KATIE

invite you to join them on the eve of their wedding
COCKTAILS • DINNER • BOWLING
Friday, June 3, 2011 • 6:30 pm • Southport Lanes & Billiards
3325 North Southport Avenue ☞ *Chicago, Illinois*

BOOK CENTERPIECES: The centerpieces were an homage to the couple's first meeting at a local coffee shop over a *Harry Potter* book, when Katherine sheepishly tried to hide the fact that she was reading a youth-inspired book, and Tristen teased her with affection. Most of the books were from their own libraries at home.

DRINK STIRRERS: The adorable drink flags were spontaneously crafted after the bride discovered a package of unused stirrers in her mother's kitchen. All in all, it was a project that took about an hour. **CLUTCH:** The bride's clutch is a vintage find from a consignment shop in Cincinnati. Katherine rediscovered it while packing for her wedding and thought it would be the perfect accessory to her gown.

PLEASE SIGN OUR *Guest Book*

hitherto

0 MADE IN CHINA

hello

Blush-hued PERFECTION

WHEN IT COMES TO WEDDINGS, whimsy means that you aren't afraid to design a day that is flirty and fun, that bucks tradition, that captures all of the idiosyncrasies of who you are as a couple. And this affair does just that. The bride stuns in a blush-hued gown, the details are simultaneously elegant and fun loving, and the style is altogether Audrey . . . Hepburn, that is.

As a single mom, Jessica, the blushing bride, waited for Mr. Right for many years. And when she found him, she knew that her wedding would be both utterly romantic *and* loads of fun. Vows were exchanged with the couple's parents and children nearby, and a celebratory cocktail party was held after the "I do's." No assigned seating or tossing of the bouquet in sight. A favorite restaurant was chosen simply because the food was loved; signature cocktails were crafted to reflect the pair's personality . . . and warmth, intimacy, and pure joy were the themes of the evening.

BRIDE & GROOM: *Jessica & Rob* • LOCATION: *San Francisco, CA* •
FLOWERS: *red dahlias, peonies, anemones, white feverfew, white and red ranunculus, beige/blush cafe au lait dahlias*

Special Touches

For my wedding dress, I chose a blush pink color because I thought it was fun and different. We chose various shades of red to coordinate with the dress. • Rob's father, a Judge, presided over our ceremony, making it so intimate. Rob spoke at the wedding and his touching toast brought everyone to tears. • At the end of the night we passed around warm beignets and dipping sauce and had a coffee and tea station with custom to-go coffee cups that said "Rob Loves Jessica."

rob
LOVES
jessica
6.11.11

WEDDING MENU: The couple opted for a menu filled with "good food over fancy," a spirit that was captured adorably with the signs their stationer crafted. From smoked ribs to macaroni-and-cheese balls, every last bit of their menu was home-inspired goodness. **WELCOME BAGS (previous spread):** All out-of-town guests were greeted by these adorable San Francisco–inspired welcome bags filled with Sun Chips, nuts, fruit bars, chocolate, wine, and water, along with a note of gratitude.

house smoked
st. louis ribs
WITH TEXAS JACK BBQ SAUCE

CAKE: The inspiration for the cake design was "simple elegance with an old-school sweetness." The same idea was used to create signature cocktails for the bride and groom: Jessica's cocktail, Sealed with a Kiss, was a mix of dark rum, pomegranate juice, lime, mint, and ginger-habañero syrup; Rob's cocktail, He Wears the Pants, was a concoction of ginger beer, vodka, fresh lime juice, and mint.

Antique CHIC

MY NEXT PICK FOR WHIMSICAL LOVELINESS is the culmination of everything I heart about being a wedding blogger. Literally. From the beautifully intimate vibe to the flirty, forever chic styling . . . from the vintage sensibility splashed so elegantly onto a clean, modern backdrop to the fun and whimsy tucked into every corner . . . from the first detail to the last, *this* is true love.

Erica and Steven knew one thing before planning their wedding: just because something was typical wedding behavior did not mean that they were going to subscribe. Instead, they wanted a day that reflected everything they loved about tying the knot: bringing together their favorite people into one room, toasting over moments that told their story—favorite foods, wines, songs, even pieces of furniture—and a general sense that they wanted to design a day from scratch that was a complete window into who they are as a couple. And the result? Well, it just might be my favorite wedding to date.

BRIDE & GROOM: *Erica & Steven* • LOCATION: *New York, NY*
• FLOWERS: *purple anemones, blue thistle, peonies, blue delphinium, lavender Lisianthus, waxflower, orange tulips, fresh lavender*

Special Touches

My father is a judge and performed a very personal but fun ceremony. He walked me down the aisle with my mom and then simply turned around and performed the ceremony that he wrote for us. • Our wedding programs were printed on popcorn bags, filled with delicious warm kettle corn, and handed out to guests along with Champagne and sparkling lemonade as they arrived. • My something new and something borrowed were fairly traditional: for something old, I tucked a vintage Polaroid of my grandparents into a gold purse that had belonged to my grandmother. And my something blue—my bridesmaids. Each maid got to choose any blue dress she wanted.

Advice

My advice is to both brides and grooms: plan the event together. It's much more fun that way, and then it's really a reflection of both of you.

––––––––––––––––––––––––––––––

"I LOVE YOU LIKE A FAT KID LOVES CAKE" PRINT: After hearing the phrase in a 50 Cent song, the bride thought it would be the perfect accessory for their dessert table. The print was gifted to her husband after the fact and now hangs in their apartment. A perfect keepsake from their sweet, whimsical day that still makes them smile.
KETTLE CORN PROGRAM BAGS (previous spread): The bags were ordered from an online coffee-supply company, then transformed into programs using a custom sticker designed by their stationer.

BOW TIES: The groom found a vendor on Etsy who was willing to craft couture bow ties for the groomsmen. He chose the fabrics, including some vintage shirts, then Erica hand sewed them. Petite versions were even crafted for the pair's six-year-old nephews. SUITCASES, VINTAGE FURNITURE, AND PROPS: The event and floral designer Hatch Creative Studio has an eclectic collection of pieces, like the vintage suitcases featured. The chairs belonged to the venue, though they were rearranged to suit the couple's unique perspective.

Charm DEFINED

THE CONCEPT OF A WHIMSICAL WEDDING can come to fruition in so many, many ways but the main component, and one that is woven throughout this next affair, is a sense of playfulness, the idea of not taking tradition too seriously. And that is exactly what I ate up by the spoonful with this next gem. It's all at once modern and romantic, yet undeniably cool and mixed with a no-holds-barred approach to color.

For Ashley and Kenny, their number one goal when planning their wedding was to create a day that celebrated their love alongside loads of laughter and lots of happy tears. They also wanted to put their own unique stamp on the day, which resulted in a killer combination that skyrocketed this fête into a whole new level of pretty whimsy. From the big, beautiful Protea blooms to the rainbow of bridesmaid shoes and the knock-your-socks-off woven fabric runners, this wedding has "unique" engraved into every single inch.

BRIDE & GROOM: *Ashley & Kenny* • LOCATION: *Los Angeles, CA*
• FLOWERS: *dahlias, peonies, air plants, King Protea, pincushion Protea, Veronica, feverfew, yarrow, ranunculus, kangaroo paw, dusty miller, astilbe, Celosia, coxcomb*

Special Touches

The floral design was based on my love for oversized, soft blooms, air plants, and vivid colors. I was pretty particular about what I wanted, down to the last bud. • Kenny made the day even more special and unique by surprising me with a song he wrote and performed during the reception.

PAPER GOODS: Dapper Paper designed the couple's invitations, marrying modern typography with a natural, organic design inspired by the wall of succulents at the reception venue.

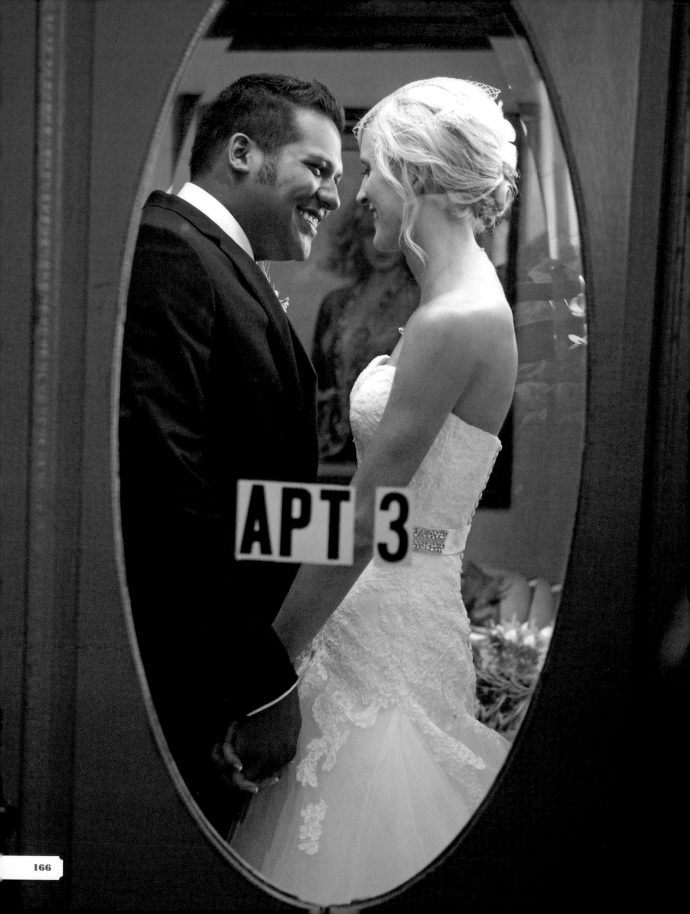

Advice Try not to get overwhelmed! I felt indecisive and confused for much of the planning process because I was inspired by so many different styles of wedding design. Try to have a plan from the beginning and stick to your guns.

BRAIDED FABRICS: Drawn to the idea of incorporating texture and color in their décor, the couple used braided fabric to create a slightly messy, pretty, and colorful look. **TERRARIUMS AND BOOK DETAILS:** Mini-terrariums were a simple way to keep the modern flora look flowing throughout the reception space. Each piece was then reused in the couple's home as a keepsake of their day.

ESCORT CARD DISPLAY: Ashley wanted a simple and modern-looking escort card display with a great font and a unique design that incorporated some of the couple's favorite plants. She loved the contrast of a crisp white pegboard with the organic nature of wood tags surrounded by beautiful greenery. **BANNERS:** Crafted by the bride from fabric remnants that she began collecting right after she said "yes," these banners were used as a backdrop for the couple's photo booth. **COFFEE WEDDING FAVORS:** Ashley and Kenny chose coffee-inspired favors to celebrate their love of the bean. The bride has a weakness for hand-stamped muslin, which happened to be the perfect way to contain the gift.

ashley & kenny's wedding

Blueprint NO 4

WHIMSICAL

FREE-SPIRITED NUPTIALS have a special place in every wedding lover's heart. It's the whimsical affairs that always leave guests buzzing, filling their minds with ideas and inspirations that they had never thought of, giving bride after bride a chance to see a day where she can kick off her heels and throw a party that is all about the fun. Yet, what really makes a whimsical wedding special and wonderfully unassuming is when style is crafted purely around personality and reflects the couple's unique relationship.

COLOR PALETTE

1 DRESS UP SIMPLE WHITE LINENS. The best part about being whimsically inclined is that you can use the base of classic pieces and add a bit of sparkle to them. Our designer chose white linen rentals, purchasing inexpensive white napkins then adding a fun and flirty tassel edge. The accents instantly turned an otherwise bland look into one that was cheerful and utterly adorable.

2 EASY-TO-FIND WICKER PLACE MATS were used to break up the whites and to add texture to the table. Guests will feel much more at home with familiar details, which means they'll be more obliged to kick back and enjoy themselves. Silver-rimmed rented plates topped our place mats, though we opted for a shape that was a bit more quirky and playful.

· TABLESCAPE ·

3 SWEET GROSGRAIN RIBBON SCRAPS kept the cutlery in place and added another element of charm.

4 COLOR IS EVERYTHING when it comes to designing a whimsically inspired space. Our centerpiece was the detail that took that color and brought it to a new level of wow, defining the palette for the entire tablescape.

5 **WHIMSY MEANS** you can really play with your design and add spunk in the most unexpected places. We stitched the guests' names onto each napkin with a supercasual script so that they served as place cards as well—a great idea for a head or sweetheart table.

· FLORALS ·

1 **WE CHOSE INCREDIBLY INEXPENSIVE STEMS**—the unjustly out-of-favor carnation—and used them in massive abundance, building a centerpiece that would take your breath away. We varied the hues, then accented them with tall pillar candles tucked into pretty silver holders.

2 **SMALL VOTIVES** were filled with just the stems of pricier blooms like peonies so that they were more visible and brought a strong feeling of luxury to the table. We also scattered some of the peonies on the table itself.

3 **FUCHSIA PEONIES** in the bouquet mimicked the texture found in the centerpiece, though on a smaller, more luxe scale. If there is one place to splurge on your florals, it's in the bridal bouquet.

CENTERPIECE FLOWERS: carnations, peonies
BOUQUET FLOWERS: peonies

1

TAKE THE CONCEPT of cake and multiply it times ten with a whimsically inspired, color-coordinated dessert bar. We chose treats that would both make the guests smile and add to the overall décor and color palette of our day.

2

CALLIGRAPHY SIGNAGE not only announced what each dessert piece was but also added a handmade feel to the table.

· CAKE ·

3

THE CAKE itself became our showstopper. Bringing in the poms from our table, the color palette of the day, and the gorgeous peony-inspired florals, the cake captured the whimsy while still being traditional and chic.

· PAPER GOODS ·

YOU ARE
CORDIALLY INVITED
TO THE WEDDING OF
Lainey Rollins
AND *Thomas Greene*
NINTH
OF JUNE 2012
SEVEN O'CLOCK IN THE EVENING
573 ROSE
LANE
LaJola
CALIFORNIA

MISS ROLLINS
TEN BLACKBIRD CIRCLE
LaJolla, California
73212

Please
SAY YES!

REPLY BY MAY 1st

MY SWEET
THOMAS
I WILL...
FOREVER
AND EVER

HEY
LAINEY,
WILL YOU
BE MY
BRIDE?

THE BRIDE +
GROOM'S
MENU

WILD MUSHROOM SOUP
WITH TRUFFLE OIL

CHILLED PETIT GREEN PEA
WATERCRESS AND CHERRY SALAD
PARMESAN
MINI
AIOLI

ROASTED   PAN ROASTED
BISON   HALIBUT
STRIPLOIN   A VANILLA SAFFRON
RED WINE AND   BEURRE BLANC
GARLIC DEMI GLACE

Cake!

1 OUR
STATIONER
employed two
major elements when crafting
the paper pieces for this fête:
calligraphy and color. Each
brightly hued piece used the
same casual, deliciously girly
calligraphy, letting guests know
that whimsy was the spirit of
the day.

2 A WHITE
PALETTE
with accents
of pink and green created
cohesion among each of the
pieces, from the invitations
themselves to the menu cards
and signage on the dessert bar.

3 THE
INVITATION
PIECES were
all typeset so that they were
slightly off center, bringing out
the childlike vibe of the art.

Al Fresco
WEDDINGS

I ADMIT, AL FRESCO ISN'T EXACTLY A DEFINED STYLE.

It's more of a feel, a vibe, if you will. But I see so many to-die-for outdoor gatherings come across my desk that I thought this variety of wedding deserved its own category— the kind of weddings that beg you to kick up your heels, toss back a glass of vino, and celebrate with the ones you love. And although Al Fresco weddings have their place mostly in mild climates, I do see brides that throw caution to the wind in all parts of the country—with a beautiful plan B, of course. After all, there is something so unbelievably romantic about sharing a fabulous meal among your nearest and dearest, dancing the night away under the stars. Add to that a strand or two of pretty twinkle lights, a deliciously unfussy menu, and a bride and groom who are glowing from the inside out, and you have a recipe for Al Fresco fabulous.

East Coast LOVELY

AS SOMEONE WHO LOOKS AT beautiful weddings day in and day out, I can honestly tell you that this particular wedding has completely and totally stolen my heart. The sweet, almost feminine styling paired with the tactile, organic touches—like a too-cute-for-words burlap banner and farm tables adorned with peonies—was every wedding lover's dream come true. It's layer upon layer of pretty with a bride and groom who literally glow.

Kimberly is a details girl. She's a blog enthusiast and someone who values the little moments that make a wedding truly spectacular. So when she and Dean set out to design their own nuptials, it was those very details that would take center stage. From programs filled with advice from grandparents, nieces, and nephews to the antique windows that were used for table assignments, every last touch was handcrafted and thoughtfully executed.

BRIDE & GROOM: *Kimberly & Dean* • LOCATION: *Westerly, RI* •
FLOWERS: *peonies, garden roses, cabbage roses, hydrangeas*

Special Touches

When guests arrived in their hotel rooms, canvas totes that said, "All you need is LOVE . . . and a little travel" awaited them. Inside were a homemade wedding survival kit, trail mix in a glass jar that said "We're nuts over you," local potato chips, water, fruit adorned with "orange you glad you're here" stickers, Duet Chocolates, and much more. We also had the hotels hang door tags that said, "All you need is LOVE . . . and a little sleep. Do not disturb, we were out celebrating with Kim & Dean all night."

Advice Don't doubt how important the little details are. At some point I was knee-deep in DIY and thought, "What am I doing? No one is going to notice these little details." But our guests raved about every last one of them.

MAZEL TOV BUNTING: The adorable handmade banner was an Etsy find. Aside from being a fabulous photo accessory, the ring bearers carried the banner behind the couple during the recessional, then placed it on the candy table for even more mileage. CAKE (following spread): The bride and groom wanted the dessert and candy bars to take center stage, so they opted for simplicity when it came to their wedding cake. Inspired by an online design, Kimberly used a simple rose pattern—a look that also happened to mimic her gown in a subtle but spectacular way.

PLEASE REPLY BY THE FIRST OF JUNE

MR. AND MRS. JOHN HAMILL
85 MEMORIAL ROAD, SUITE 501
WEST HARTFORD, CONNECTICUT 06107

MR. AND MRS. JOHN HAMILL
MRS. BARBARA MATUS
MR. ALAN MATUS
REQUEST THE HONOUR OF YOUR PRESENCE
AT THE MARRIAGE OF THEIR CHILDREN

Kimberly

AND

Dean

SUNDAY, THE TWENTY-SIXTH OF JUNE
TWO THOUSAND ELEVEN
AT FIVE O'CLOCK
SHELTER HARBOR GOLF CLUB
CHARLESTOWN, RHODE ISLAND

BLACK TIE INVITED

PRETTY IN *Pink*

BREATHLESS. THIS WEDDING WILL LEAVE YOU BREATHLESS.
In fact, it just might find you ditching all of your wedding must-haves to date and plowing full force ahead into a fête Just. Like. This. And whether or not you have the luxury of tying the knot in perfectly perfect weather, or the funds to deck out your day in the most beautiful peonies a girl could ever want, remember that tucked inside each flawless image is a style that is simply girl, with pretty pinks taking center stage and a garden-inspired style that will leave your hearts aflutter. And that, my lovelies, is *so* doable.

BRIDE & GROOM: *Lulu & Gavin* • LOCATION: *Santa Barbara, CA*
• FLOWERS: *pink and coral charm peonies, hot pink garden roses (Maria Theresa and Darcy), garden roses*

Special Touches

We are both very close to our families and did not want our wedding to be just the union of two people, but the union of two families and cultures. Gavin's uncle, our officiant, learned Chinese phrases to incorporate into our ceremony. • Dinner filled with candlelight, blooming florals, and laughing friends were perhaps the most special of touches. My father's heartfelt speech to his only child and seeing him cry for the first time in my life. My aunt and uncle, who flew across the world to be there, and Skyping Gavin's grandmother in for the ceremony! We were simply overwhelmed by it all.

FORTUNE COOKIES AND FAVORS: Friends and family shared their "Tips for Happily Ever After" on sheets of paper inserted into pink-paper fortune cookies. (A few gems: "When arguing, you have a choice. You can be right, or you can be happy" and "Don't stop being newlyweds!") Wedding favors were handmade bride-and-groom chocolate truffles created by the Bacara's pastry chef. The bride truffles were decorated with lace white dresses and the groom truffles sported tuxedos. The chef even made the bow ties on the groom truffles pink to match Gavin's! **FLOWERS:** With a father who is a botanist, Lulu grew up surrounded by beautiful flowers. Thus, from the moment she said "I will," she knew what she wanted—pink peonies, roses, and ranunculus for their soft, romantically ruffled edges. Peonies are the traditional Chinese wedding flowers, so the stem fit the bill to perfection.

CAKE: The bride and groom both have a sweet tooth and simply couldn't choose just one flavor for their wedding cake . . . so they picked three! The cake was layered with tiramisu, red velvet, and berries with Bavarian cream.

Wine Country
STYLE

WHEN IT COMES TO WEDDINGS, the wineries in Santa Ynez exude sweeping beauty, sophistication, and total style. There is such an innate sense of loveliness built into the backdrop, the weddings held in this region tend to blend seamlessly onto that canvas. This next little number is textured, layered, and overflowing with complete, unabashed pretty that captures the Wine Country style flawlessly.

When the bride is a wedding planner, the bar for her own wedding suddenly becomes very high, though Kim and her fiancé, Kevin, knew two things for sure: they wanted their outdoor wedding to feel simultaneously casual and timelessly elegant. Roblar Winery in Santa Ynez proved to be the perfect backdrop to infuse their rich, eclectic aesthetic. Using a set of teal vases that their designer found, they layered in a collection of milk glass, mercury glass, and a palette of warm oranges, yellows, and reds.

BRIDE & GROOM: *Kim & Kevin* • LOCATION: *Santa Ynez, CA* •
FLOWERS: *herbs such as sage and rosemary, dahlias, yellow yarrow, ranunculus*

Special Touches

After the ceremony, guests moved to a great lawn where everyone enjoyed "His" and "Hers" stations. I am allergic to shellfish and Kevin is allergic to dairy, so we decided to do a fun play on this with the bars. I had a gourmet cheese station that would make any monger proud and Kevin had a raw bar that I was not allowed near. • We matched each bar with fun His/Hers cocktails—Heirloom Bloody Marys with the raw bar and a Summer Melon Sour for Hers. We also had a tasting bar showcasing all of Roblar's wines.

Tonight's Menu

Heirloom Tomato & Avocado Napoleon
SLICED HEIRLOOM TOMATOES STACKED BETWEEN LAYERS OF THINLY SLICED AVOCADO
DRESSED WITH A LIGHT VINAIGRETTE ON BED OF LOCAL GREENS
SERVED WITH 2008 SANTA BARBARA COUNTY SAUVIGNON BLANC

Timbale of Local Halibut Tarta
CUCUMBER AND FENNEL
SERVED WITH 2008 O PESCADOR

Braised Beef Short Ribs
MARINATED AND SLOWLY BRAISED IN A PROVENÇALE DAUBE, SERVED WITH
GARLIC MASHED POTATOES, SAUTÉED SPINACH
SERVED WITH 2008 SYRAH

Dessert, The Sweet Stuff
TRIO OF SORBET - SANTA ROSA PLUM, FRESH PEACH AND WHITE NECTARINE
SERVED WITH CHOCOLATE TORTE ON A LOCAL RASPBERRY MERLOT SAUCE

To our Meat-Free Friends, please let your server know.

Let's feast!

His

Raw Bar
Selection of oysters, shrimp, rock
crab claws & uni shooters

His Cocktail
Heirloom Bloody Mary
Soju with homemade heirloom
tomato mix & local olives

COLOR PALETTE: The color palette started with the invitations. Stationer Bridget Williams pulled together pieces using orange and shades of blue. Meg from La Partie Events brought the palette to life through the selected florals and their vessels. **FLORALS AND DÉCOR:** Teal vases found by the designer were used as a design launching pad. When they were paired with the designer's collection of vintage milk-glass vases and some mercury-glass candleholders, the result was warm and textured and full of color. **PAPER GOODS:** The invitations and paper accoutrements balanced whimsy with tradition. Although the invitations themselves were quite classic, the accompanying pieces like the Mexican Fiesta rehearsal invite and the "attire" card (letting guests know what to wear to each of the events) were quite casual. The balance reflected the mood of the entire weekend.

LANTERNS: Found via Lazy Susan USA, these lanterns brought a worldly element to the décor, grounding the reception tables and giving them a stunning focal point. **PIÑATA GIFT BAGS:** Given out at the rehearsal dinner, each bag was hand stamped and designed to match the rehearsal invite. **COOKIE FAVOR BAGS:** Each bag, made to fill with cookies, included a cookie-inspired quote printed on kraft paper.

Hers
Cocktail

SUMMER MELON SOUR
SOJU WITH MELON
INFUSED BRANDY & LIME

Blueprint NO **5**

AL FRESCO

THE SECRET SAUCE to planning an Al Fresco wedding is ambience—creating an environment that feels warm and welcoming, that begs your guests to stay a little while longer and pour a second (or fourth) glass of wine. At their very core, these celebrations should be inviting and inspired by home. By approaching this type of design as you would your home décor, you'll give yourself permission to think creatively when it comes to each element. Thus, for our Al Fresco Blueprint, we loved the idea of repurposing household items to evoke a sense of intimacy.

COLOR PALETTE

1

EDIBLE FAVORS

are a beautiful way to give your guests a meaningful, home-style takeaway. We wrapped rustic baguettes in paper, then tied them with twine. Simple but delicious.

2

THE OUTDOORS CAN be as understated or as bold as you want. Don't be afraid to infuse your décor with color; pairing a vibrant hue on top of a vibrant one really complements the whole Al Fresco style.

3

ADD IN LOTS OF TEXTURE, reminding guests of dining in your home. Think macramé, inspired patterns and prints, tactile fabrics. For a runner, our designer actually used inexpensive rugs from Urban Outfitters.

· TABLESCAPE ·

1 THERE IS NO NEED TO
BE TIMID when choosing
flowers for your Al Fresco
centerpieces. Whatever the color, whatever the
style, aim to infuse a bit of handpicked goodness
into each piece. Quick tip . . . grab some shears
and head over to the closest garden. Tuck your
fresh-from-the-garden flowers into small vases to
accent the professionally crafted pieces.

· FLORALS ·

2 GO AU NATUREL. Wood
vases and branch slices bring the
beauty of nature to the table. No
vases? No problem! Bright blossoms
look great all on their own spread along the table.

3 FOR THE BRIDAL
BOUQUET, think about texture.
We used dahlias, zinnias, ranunculus,
wild grasses, and lavender.

CENTERPIECE FLOWERS: marigolds, ranunculus, zinnias, wild grasses, and lavender · BOUQUET FLOWERS: dahlias, zinnias, ranunculus, wild grasses, and lavender

1 CHOOSE ONE DOMINANT COLOR

(turquoise, in this case) to showcase. Pick accompanying colors that blend well and don't compete with the rest of the cake. Hand-painted detailing is a beautiful way to bring in that pop of color without overwhelming the design.

· CAKE ·

2 TURN TO FASHION

for inspiration. This cake was inspired by a bridal headpiece.

3 TO CAPTURE the Al

Fresco style, bring the element of nature into your design. For this cake, a light brown sugar flower ties in to the wood detailing seen in the vases and burlap on the table.

1 AL FRESCO-INSPIRED DESIGNS

blend together artisanal, romantic, and creative elements. We wanted to infuse that handmade touch while retaining a thoughtfully crafted, somewhat classic style. Try to think of the typography as its own form of art.

2 ESTABLISH A COMMON THREAD that

can easily weave through all paper goods. Here it was Indian folk art for our Indian bride. Nothing should be uniform. Instead, the pieces should meander, ramble, tell a story from one to the next.

· PAPER GOODS ·

3 LOOK FOR INSPIRATION from

vintage graphics and patterns abroad. We found ours in textiles from Mexico, Sri Lanka, and India, all of which have amazing antique patterns. In this suite, we focused on the Indian folk art, drawing a flower pattern to suggest wildflower fields.

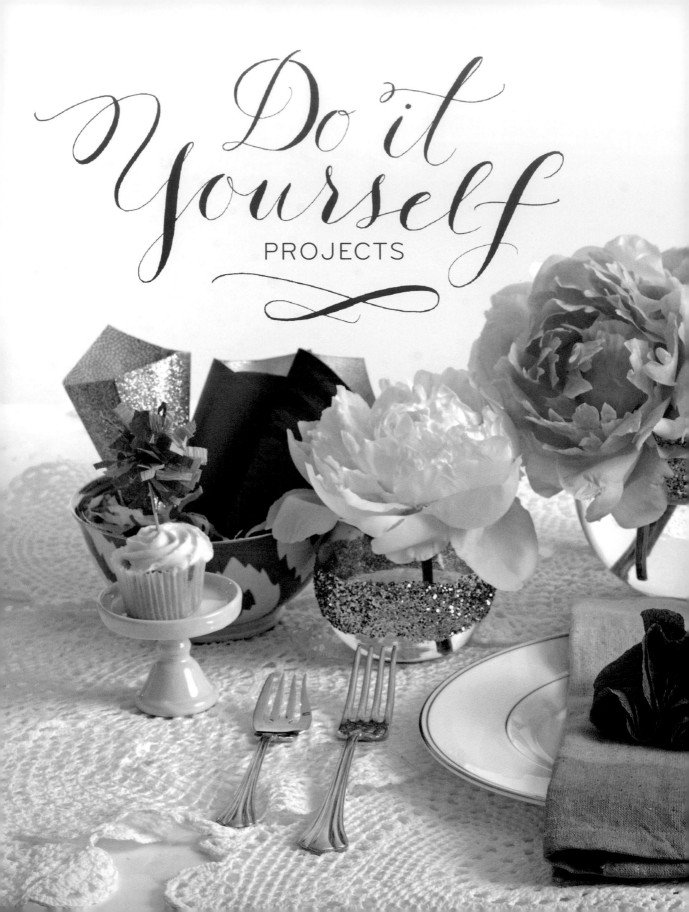

Do it Yourself
PROJECTS

DIY IS A FRAME OF MIND. And it can be as simple or as complex as you make it. Though for the truly exquisite bespoke celebrations, from million-dollar to budget fêtes alike, DIY is nearly a requirement. Whether it's a handwritten note at each place setting, crepe paper blooms that adorn your favor boxes, or something entirely new that you've dreamed up . . . each and every wedding should have a "special something" that sets it apart from all the rest. I believe it's these personal touches infused into your day that transform an ordinary affair into one of which dreams are made. But here's the real key: learning to edit yourself is the most invaluable DIY skill a girl could ever have. Choose only the ideas that truly elevate your design. Carefully curate your projects to those that are fun and add to the enjoyment of planning your big day. And unless you are a born DIY-er, avoid the chaos that is sure to ensue if you attempt to handcraft your entire affair. So in the celebration of all things Do It Yourself, I've compiled fifteen supersimple projects for you to fall in love with, projects that will add prettiness and charm to any affair, that will elevate your wedding design to unforgettable status. And rest assured, even novice crafters will find these projects not only doable but also must-have-able!

Some are projects that you've never seen before. Some are fresh takes on old classics. Each design that we've crafted is made to stand alone or to work as part of a collection. The décor elements blend beautifully with the favor packaging. The cake topper looks stunning next to the gussied-up vases. They are crafted so that each and every project complements the next with the intention that . . .

1 you see how versatile your raw materials can really be,
2 you save money buying materials that can be mixed and matched, and used for a variety of different applications,
3 you see the cohesion and style that can come by using a distinctive group of colors, prints, patterns, and textures.

The projects that I've chosen are fun and modern and fresh, rooted in beautiful wedding tradition. I hope to illustrate that by simply changing the color paper or the type of fabric used on a tried-and-true idea, you'll be able to design a collection of details that will fit seamlessly into your own unique wedding.

Tassel Cake Bunting

WE'VE ALL SEEN BUNTING-INSPIRED CAKE TOPPERS.

In fact, it just might be the most adorable DIY project to ever come out of the World Wide Web. Inspired by a crepe paper tassel I found on the *Oh Happy Day* blog, my team of editors and I gussied up the classic bunting a bit, making a design that is both festive and undeniably cute. Stick with our pink and red palette or mix and match different crepe paper hues to come up with your own superfun look.

Crepe paper, A.C. Moore
(we used three different hues,
1 sheet of each hue)

Jute packaging, 50 yards

Scissors or paper cutter

Glue gun

Twine, Michaels

2 12-inch skewers, A.C. Moore

2-tiered cake (6-inch top and
9-inch base), Whole Foods

· STYLE TIP ·

*I like these best when tucked neatly
into a seriously simple white cake.
I scored this two-tiered beauty at
Whole Foods for less than $50!*

1. Cut your crepe paper into 8 to 10 × ¼-inch shreds. We used a paper cutter, which made this step superfast.

2. Gather your crepe paper so that you have one long bunch, holding the center with two fingers. About 1 inch on either side of the center, begin twisting the paper tightly.

3. Make a small loop with the twisted portion, ensuring that you keep your twist tight.

4. Twist the loop clockwise so that it stays in place. We wrapped a piece of crepe paper around this portion and secured it with a dot of hot glue, though it isn't necessary. Trim your strands so that the crepe paper tassel is the length you like.

5. Follow the above steps to make 6 more tassels.

6. Knot a 16-inch (give or take) piece of twine to the top of one of your skewers. Trim the bit of excess twine from your knot and secure it with a dot of glue.

7. Thread your tassels onto your length of twine, spacing them about 1 inch apart and securing the crepe paper to the twine with a dot of glue. Repeat with the remaining tassels until you have secured the desired number.

8. Tie the loose end of twine to your second 12-inch skewer and knot it, trim it, then secure to the second skewer with a dot of hot glue.

9. Place the skewers gently in your cake, ensuring that they are inserted at least 2 inches deep.

Crepe Paper Cupcake Pom

SINCE THE GIRLS AND I had a bit of leftover crepe paper from
our tassel bunting project, we decided to craft these too-cute-for-words
cupcake poms. It was a crazy-easy, crazy-inexpensive project that thrilled
us with its impact. Debut on a dessert table alongside your tassel cake
bunting, and you have the recipe for total delight!

Crepe paper, A.C. Moore (we used three different hues leftover from cake bunting)

Twine, Michaels

Wooden craft picks

Scissors

· STYLE TIP ·

I adore the idea of dipping your wooden pick in gold leaf paint, then topping with an all-white crepe paper pom. It's a superchic approach for this otherwise charming project.

1 Cut the crepe paper into 6 × ¼-inch long strips.

2 Gather the crepe paper, holding the center with two fingers.

3 Tightly tie an 8-inch piece of twine around the center of your crepe paper.

4 Holding the twine-and-pom combo horizontally, tie the twine around the top of your wooden craft pick and secure as tightly as possible with a knot.

5 Repeat steps 1 through 3 to create a second small pom.

6 Tie your second pom to the stick, alternating the direction you tie the twine so that the pom fills up the open space. Your two pieces of twine should be tied criss-crossed in somewhat of an *X*.

7 Twist and fluff gently. Trim to ensure that the crepe paper is even all the way around. Secure both poms to the stick with a small dab of hot glue spread thinly over the back pieces of twine.

Paper Cones

THE RICE TOSS—still one of my all-time favorite wedding traditions, with its many fun alternatives—is a wedding must-have. Gussying up this classic accoutrement by simply choosing a variety of different papers, then completing the look with a gorgeous metallic liner, is a surefire way to bring your guests a big smile for the cameras and a splash of style to your wedding day décor. We filled our cones with crepe paper shreds left over from the tassel bunting and cupcake pom projects, though they would be absolutely darling with ice cream sprinkles or lavender. The best thing about this DIY project is that by simply switching up the papers, you can truly complement any wedding style.

Handmade papers: hot pink current fine paper, Lokta bean white, gold on cream mums, Lokta white raised damask, and Ferro gold, from Paper Source (most papers were approximately 20 × 30 inches; you can also opt for the 12 × 12-inch scrapbook paper)

Wrapping papers: We used a gold glitter roll and a P.S. strawberry roll, from Paper Source. As an alternative, you can use inexpensive text-weight decorative paper.

Ruler

Paper cutter or scissors

Super Tacky Tape (½-inch width), Paper Source (glue guns and other double-stick tapes work well, too)

Filling of choice

1. Cut your papers into 6-inch squares. You'll need an outside paper and a liner, so two 6-inch squares for each cone.

2. Using the double-stick tape on one edge of the 6-inch square, adhere the two sheets together back to back. After you have the two sheets adhered on one edge, use your hand to mock the roll that you will be making with the cone, then adhere the second edge. (This will help to prevent wrinkling in the paper when you roll it.)

3. Turn your paper over and apply one strip of tape to the liner side. If you are using a glue gun, skip this step.

4. With the tape side away from you, hold your paper so that a corner is pointed up. Bring the adjacent corner across the cone to roll it. Bring the other corner across and secure with the placed double-sided tape or a line of hot glue. If using tape, a small dot of hot glue will help to ensure that your cone doesn't come unwrapped.

5. Fill with pom-poms, crepe paper shreds, or lavender!

· STYLE TIP ·

To achieve a more classic look, go for a white exterior in something fun like a lace paper, then line with silver. The handmade papers that I used were pricey, but by mixing in some more economical options, including wrapping papers, they were still quite budget friendly.

When you're crafting these, though, don't forget to think about sweet Mother Nature and fill them with all things biodegradable.

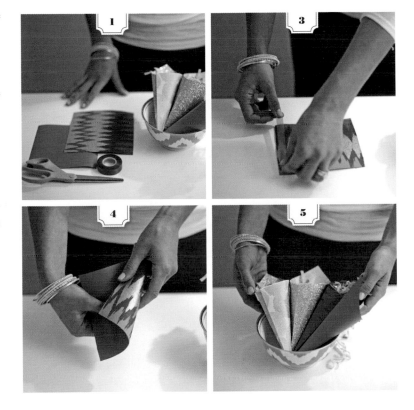

Doily Overlay

AHHH, THE DOILY. Thanks in large part to wedding and design blogs, you may have seen lots of doily goodness happening lately. And yet amid all of the pretty I've spotted online, I really wanted to push the doily to an even prettier place. This doily table cover is a décor accessory with the perfect combination of vintage and modern charm! Whether used as an overlay on a simple white linen tablecloth or draped over a wooden farm table, the goal was for our finished product to make even the most experienced design gurus swoon. Size-wise, our table cover ended up being about 48 × 84 inches, though yours will ultimately depend on the size and placement of the doilies.

Large embroidered doilies (14 to 16 inches), Jo-Ann Fabric

Small embroidered doilies (10 to 11 inches), Jo-Ann Fabric

Hot glue gun (or needle and thread)

· STYLE TIP ·

Using a ³/₄ sugar plus ¹/₄ water solution, you can stiffen this overlay and craft your own altar backdrop. Hung on a wooden wall, a black panel, or from a stunning old tree, this would be such a gorgeous detail to have when exchanging vows.

1 Determine your desired length and width. Starting with the larger doilies, begin laying them out so that they hug each other with only a slight overlap. We used three large doilies for our width of approximately 48 inches. Because we purchased a hodgepodge of sizes, and even slightly varying shapes, our spacing was a bit irregular. We used 10 to 12 larger doilies per row, though we also left some intentional gaps. To me, the gaps were part of the charm!

2 Move around the doilies until you find the perfect fit for each one, taking care not to overcrowd the piece as a whole. All in all, our project required a total of 26 doilies.

3 Where they overlap, glue them together (or sew with blind stitches, knotting on the back). Allow to dry completely, then stand back and admire your masterpiece!

Note: Make sure to cover your workspace with a plastic tarp, newspaper, or an old bedsheet to protect your surface.

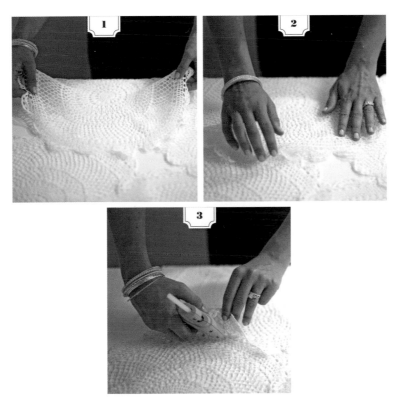

Glittered Vase

I'M ALWAYS LOOKING FOR INEXPENSIVE WAYS TO

spruce up a plain but useful vase. I probably shouldn't admit this, but I have been known to "alter" my nana's inexpensive clear vases to give them a little more zing. (With eight children and twenty-something grandkids, she accumulated a lot of, dare I say, cheap vases.) Enter a trusty bottle of glitter and invisible glue. This project takes two minutes soup to nuts (not including drying time) and makes for a beautiful keepsake. I, personally, prefer them lined up in a nice crisp row down the center of a long head table, filled to the brim with peonies, but there are about a million places and spaces you'll need these pretty little pops of flowers.

Bubble bowls, Michaels

Art glitter adhesive, Paper Source

Small bowl, for glue

1-inch paintbrush

Large bowl, for catching glitter

Gold glitter

Aluminum foil or plastic wrap
(optional)

Krylon Glitter Blast, Michaels

1 Pour your glue into a small bowl for easy access.

2 Paint a 1- to 2-inch strip of glue around the top or center of your
bubble bowl, varying the placement from bowl to bowl.

3 Holding your vase over a large bowl, sprinkle the glitter around the
vase until all the glue is completely covered. Your bowl should catch
the glitter that doesn't stick for use on your next vase.

4 Set aside to let dry while you complete the remaining vases.

5 If desired, once your vases are completely dry, wrap the unglittered
portion tightly in aluminum foil or plastic wrap. Then spray your glitter
with the glitter blast (this will ensure that glitter doesn't fall off during
transport). Let dry and remove the foil or plastic.

· STYLE TIP ·

*Try using clear sequins for a more
textured effect. Surrounded by
votive candles, these beauties
will be romantic and sparkly.
Instead of flowers, you could place
inexpensive candles in the vases.
The glow would be magical.*

FLOWER GIRL
White Ribbon Wand

OKAY, SO RIBBON WANDS FOR YOUR FLOWER GIRL
isn't exactly a novel idea. But when you up the style ante on this tried-and-true
detail, you will turn cheesy into L-O-V-E. Rich, dreamy ribbon is the deal maker
for ribbon wands. The key: find ribbons in different textures and styles, while
keeping to one monochromatic hue. The result is a super-duper fun detail that
will leave your guests, not to mention your sweet flower girl, grinning all night
long. Plus, your little maid can take this home as her own special keepsake to
remember the day that she got to be a real fairy princess.

White ribbons in varying textures and widths, all from Michaels (we used 1-inch pom-pom ribbon, 2-inch satin ribbon, 1-inch grosgrain, ½-inch grosgrain, and ½-inch satin)

Scissors

⁷⁄₁₆-inch dowell rods, Michaels

Twine, Michaels

Glue gun

· STYLE TIP ·

Play with color to fit this too-cute-for-words detail into the style of your wedding. Although I used a white palette, I was also dreaming of pinks and yellows to add a bit of spunk. Or gold. I could die happy seeing a flower girl walk down the aisle with a golden ribbon wand. This is one Do It Yourself project where you can really let your imagination shine through. Another idea: make miniature versions of the wands for all of your guests, placing them on the ceremony chairs. The photo op of your guests waving the wands in celebration will be priceless!

1 Cut your ribbon to about 30 inches long. You need between 6 and 12 strips.

2 Gather all of your ribbons, holding them in the center with two fingers. Tie a piece of twine tightly around the center of the ribbons.

3 Place the dowel rod against the twine.

4 Select one of the ribbons that is close to the dowel and tie that tightly around the dowel. Knot to secure, then tuck a small dot of hot glue under the ribbon onto the dowel and press your knot against it.

5 Optional: To cover the place where you've attached the ribbon, consider adding a bow or other accessory like a vintage brooch. Just be sure to use a superstrong glue if it's the least bit heavy.

Ombré Napkins

& PAPER GOODS

RIT DYE IS DEFINITELY A DIY TOOL KIT ESSENTIAL.

This inexpensive solution allows you to get crazy-creative with color and texture, essentially designing entirely new looks for just about any fabric or paper element. We're pairing a little bit of Rit Dye with some muslin napkins (we stitched ours up quickly from a few yards of natural muslin, though you can also score inexpensive varieties at budget retailers such as IKEA and Target). The goal was to create a vibrant, watercolor-inspired ombré effect. This graduated hue was easy-peasy to do, and aside from the drying time, only took about twelve minutes per napkin. With enough friends, Tupperware, and bottles of wine, it makes for a pretty festive evening!

Large Tupperware container

Water

Rubber gloves

Liquid Rit Dye in petal pink and fuchsia, Michaels

Unbleached cotton muslin fabric, Jo-Ann Fabric

---

1 Fill a large Tupperware container with 4 inches (about 1 or 2 gallons depending on the size of your container) of water. Donning the gloves, pour in 2 tablespoons of petal pink and 1 tablespoon of fuchsia dye (less for a lighter ombré, more for a darker ombré effect). Stir well with a large spoon.

2 Note where you want the ombré to end, and saturate the napkin beneath that area completely in clear water. Wring gently to transport.

3 Slowly dip your napkin up to the point where you want your ombré to end (where your waterline ends). Pull right back up out of the dye, leaving about 2 inches of your napkin submersed in the liquid.

4 Let the bottom 2 inches soak in your dye for 10 minutes, then remove.

5 Hang to dry (I just draped mine over the Tupperware so that any drips went back into the basin) overnight. The dye will drift up your napkin to create the ombré effect.

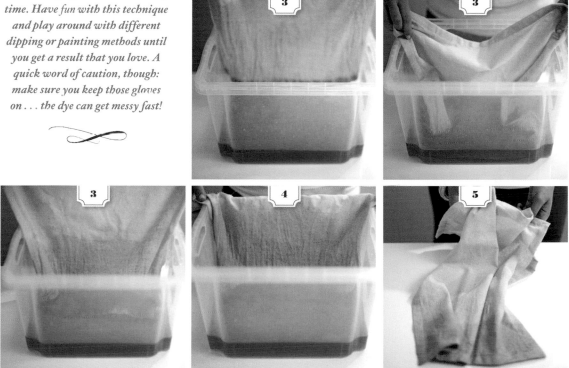

~ NO 8 ~

YARN-WRAPPED
Water / Wine Bottle

IF EVER THERE WAS A PROJECT THAT EVEN
the most timid DIY hopeful could do, this would be it. We found a few
inexpensive wine bottles, a couple of pretty table numbers, some pink
yarn, and voilà. A ridiculously easy project done in no time at all!

Liquid leaf in classic gold, Michaels

½-inch paintbrush

Wooden number, Michaels

34-ounce square hermetic bottle, Container Store

Red Heart Designer Sport Yarn in blush rose and girlie pink, around 2 to 3 yards, A.C. Moore

Glue gun

Scissors

· STYLE TIP ·

No need to include a table number. These can be used to serve wine, water, or lemonade, lining the tables with a bit of handmade goodness. Choose yarn that fits the style of your wedding, and you have absolute DIY perfection.

1 Paint your number gold using the gold leaf paint and a small paintbrush (½ inch or so). Allow it to dry completely.

2 Hold the yarn vertically on the wine bottle about 3 inches from the bottom of the bottle. Wrap the yarn around the bottle a few times, overlapping the vertical piece of yarn to make sure the yarn stays put.

3 Continue coiling the yarn around the bottle. Make sure to wrap tightly, pushing the layers close together.

4 When you've reached the desired height, hot glue the end of the yarn to the back of the bottle. Trim off any extra.

5 To create a striped effect, continue with a different color just as you did above.

6 Apply hot glue to the back of your number, then place it on top of the yarn on the side without seams. Hold in place until secure.

CHALKBOARD HEART
Escort Cards

DURING MY DIY ADVENTURES, I stumbled upon the most adorable crafter ever. Kelsey, designer behind the Etsy shop Twisted Twig, conceptualized these darling escort cards for me, and the minute I laid eyes on them, I was hooked. Using 29¢ hearts she found at Michaels, a little chalkboard paint, and some cute poms—even leftover varieties from your cupcake pom project would work—led to the most fabulously inexpensive presentation for an otherwise kind of boring detail. Love, love, love.

Wooden hearts, Michaels

Newspaper or tarp

Krylon chalkboard spray paint, A.C. Moore

Glue gun

Colorful poms, A.C. Moore

White Chalk Ink marker, Michaels

· STYLE TIP ·

For a splurge, have your calligrapher write the names using a pretty white chalk pen. This instantly becomes a perfect keepsake for your guests! Or attach them to glittered clothespins (crafted by painting one side with glue, then covering in glitter) and hang them from a piece of ribbon or twine.

1 Lay out the hearts on the tarp or newspaper. Completely coat one side with the chalkboard paint and allow to dry completely.

2 Repeat on the opposite side. You might need to repeat this process for full coverage.

3 Make sure the sides are coated as well, so that the entire heart is covered in chalkboard paint. Allow to dry completely.

4 Using a dab of hot glue, adhere your poms to the top left or right corner.

5 The Chalk Ink marker will allow you to write the names on the hearts in a calligraphy style.

~ NO 10 ~

Heart Garland

ONCE KELSEY OF TWISTED TWIG got started helping me with wedding DIY projects, it was impossible for me to let her go. As we were talking through ideas, Kelsey showed us an incredible, glittery garland chandelier that she had crafted. I loved the idea, though it was important to me to put our own spin on it. So instead, I took that same garland concept and draped it from the back of a dining chair. You've undoubtedly seen the ribbon detailing popularized in the last few years. And you know we love all things ribbon. But these paper hearts—just too cute. What looked like such an intimidating project turned out to be so easy, I jumped to include it in this book.

Tacky glue spray, Michaels

Fuchsia cover stock, Paper Source

Gold glitter wrapping paper, Paper Source

Fiskars large (2-inch) heart craft punch, Michaels

Sewing machine

Thread, either in a neutral hue like ecru or a hue designed to match your hearts

Fishing wire

· STYLE TIP ·

Hang these from a painted gold branch or PVC pipe and use as a backdrop for your dessert table. The more hearts you include, the more fabulous it becomes!

1 Using the spray adhesive, adhere one piece of card stock to the wrapping paper. The heavyweight cover stock paper plus the lighter weight wrapping paper should easily work with your craft punch. Two cover stock papers might be difficult to punch.

2 Using your heart punch, punch away. We used anywhere from 15 to 25 hearts per strand, varying the length of each strand.

3 Run your hearts through the sewing machine, leaving 1 to 2 centimeters of thread between each heart. This is not an exact science and will still look great if your lines are crooked or you don't have even spacing between your hearts.

4 To drape on a chair, punch a hole at the very top of your uppermost heart, then thread your fishing wire through, tying around the top of the chair and knotting securely.

Glittered Letters

I MAY BE STARTING TO SOUND like a broken "this is easy" record, but when it comes to this next project, I literally couldn't resist. It was, bar none, our simplest DIY, and the result just happened to pack the most wow factor of any of the projects. I found the letters at Jo-Ann's, covered them in glue, then sprinkled them with glitter. DIY for Dummies might be a better title for this project . . . though the result was way too cute to call it that.

Paintbrush

8-inch papier-mâché letters,
Jo-Ann Fabrics

12-inch papier-mâché letters,
Jo-Ann Fabrics

Mod Podge, Michaels

Tupperware or bowl

Creatology gold glitter, Michaels

Tarp or bedsheet (optional)

Krylon Glitter Blast, Michaels

· STYLE TIP ·

*Even just dipping the tips of the
cardboard letters turned out to be
completely adorable. I prefer the
larger-scale glitter to the more
dusty variety as the shimmer and
shine really takes these to a level
of love. But it's totally personal
preference when it comes to
creating your own look. You could
even mimic the ombré effect that
we used in our napkins (page 226)
by using a spectrum of dark to
light glitter hues.*

1 Paint the letter with Mod Podge so that the front portion is entirely covered.

2 Holding the letter over the bowl, sprinkle the glitter over every part of the glue so that the entire front of the letter is coated in glitter. Set aside and allow to dry completely. The fallen glitter can be reused on your next letter. Note: A tarp or an old bedsheet placed on the table is a great way to catch stray glitter so that your floor doesn't sparkle too.

3 Depending on your style, you can either leave the back of the letter uncoated or you can finish it off with more glue and glitter. It's messy, but *so* worth it.

4 After the letters have dried, coat with a layer of Glitter Blast to ensure that most of the glitter stays put.

Paper-Wrapped Letters

USING THE GLITTER LETTERS AS A LAUNCHING PAD,

Kelscy inspired this paper-covered variety. I could hardly believe how awesome the result is, all with a little bit of glue and a piece of lovely handmade paper. The real beauty in this project lies in its versatility. Choose more classic papers for an elegant look; go for a big bold print for a more modern variety. The options are endless!

8-inch papier-mâché letters,
Jo-Ann Fabrics

Hot pink current fine paper, Paper
Source

Pencil

Scissors

Mod Podge, Michaels

½- or 1-inch paintbrush

Emery board or nail file (optional)

· STYLE TIP ·

*I love letters placed on dessert
tables, hanging off the bride's and
groom's chair, as photo-booth
accessories, or used to gussy up a
guest-book table. Think creatively
with the words and letters you
choose: xoxo, smooch, kiss, forever,
and love are among my faves.*

1 Trace your letter onto the back of the paper and cut it out.

2 Paint Mod Podge onto the front of the papier-mâché letter.

3 Adhere the cut-out paper letter onto the papier-mâché letter. Allow it
to dry completely.

4 Smooth the edges with an emery board or nail file if desired.

MR. & MRS.

Wrapped Hangers

INSTEAD OF THE CLASSIC "BRIDE AND GROOM" hanging over the sweetheart chairs, we love the idea of using these *Mr.* and *Mrs.* yarn-wrapped hangers. They take a little muscle and a good eye, but the result is a keepsake you'll treasure. After all is said and done, hang these babies over your bedside tables to remind yourselves of your big day.

Red Heart Designer Sport Yarn in girlie pink, A.C. Moore

Wire hanger

Pliers

Wire cutters

Yarn

Scissors

Glue gun

· STYLE TIP ·

For a more modern or elegant look, try wrapping with a beautiful velvet ribbon. For a rustic look, go for twine.

1 Unravel the wire hanger and bend and shape it into the word of your choice. This takes a bit of patience, but with the pliers you should be able to fashion the hanger into any old word you please.

2 Cut off any unused wire ends using the wire cutters.

3 Starting at one end, begin wrapping the wire tightly with yarn, overlapping the first few wraps to secure.

4 When you have completely wrapped the wire, cut the yarn and fasten it into place with a dash of hot glue.

Note: If you want to use the ampersand in between your letters, refer back to our Paper-Wrapped Letters project (page 236) or coat a simple cardboard & in pretty paint or glitter—or leave it as is!

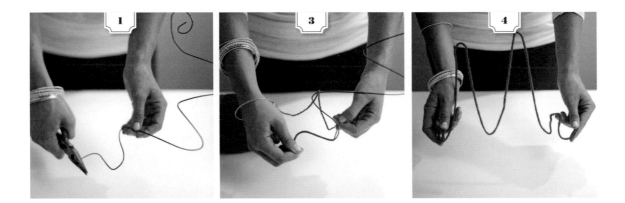

Crepe Paper Flowers

ONCE I MASTERED THE ART OF FABRIC FLOWERS,

I went back to the ease of creating those same blooms with paper, proven gorgeous by the girls at Posh Paperie in one of their beloved DIY projects on Style Me Pretty. The best part? These little gems are so easy and require nothing more than a bit of paper and some twine. Plus, they happen to be one of the most versatile projects in wedding DIY-land. We used three of these babies to top our clear favor box, though you could also adorn a simple white napkin, gussy up an escort card, or elevate your menu to a place of fabulous. There are so many ways to use this project, it's almost a no-brainer.

Crepe paper in Bombay, A.C. Moore (we used three different hues)

3.5 × 3.5 × 3.5-inch clear box

Ruler

Scissors

Twine, Michaels

Hot glue gun

· STYLE TIP ·

Try using three or four different hues of paper to create an ombré flower. Tie them around your flower girl's wrist with a piece of twine or tuck one into her bun, and you have the most adorable, affordable accessory ever.

1 Cut four 6 × 6-inch crepe paper squares, laying them each on top of one another.

2 Fold the stack of paper in half.

3 Cut a semicircle starting at the right side of the fold. As you cut, make subtle petal shapes.

4 Unfold and layer the pieces on top of each other so that the petals are facing different directions.

5 Fold the stack in half, then pinch in each side toward the center.

6 Gather the base and tie a piece of twine around it.

7 Fluff the petals so that they resemble a flower.

8 Hot glue them to your favor packaging. We bundled three together for a more dramatic look.

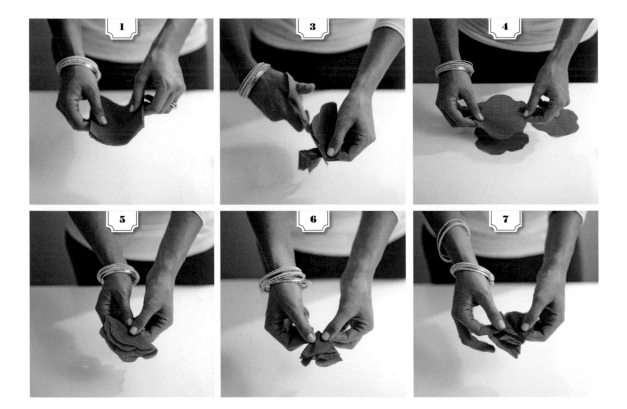

Linen Favor Bags

ANY TIME I SEE A SEWING MACHINE INCLUDED IN
a Do It Yourself project, I tend to run the other way. But before you do, take my
word for it: from one sewing-challenged girl to the next, these linen favor bags are
a snap. You don't even have to sew a straight line to make them cute. The beauty is
in the imperfections and in crafting a series of bags that look lovely together or on
their own. Fill with sweets, coffee beans, or a cute note of thanks. It's these little
touches that lend meaning to a bespoke wedding. One yard of fabric makes about
eight bags, with plenty of "mistake space," though you can squeeze more in if you're
experienced with a sewing machine.

Linen, found on sale at Jo-Ann Fabrics

Ruler

Scissors

Sewing machine

White or ecru thread

Unbleached cotton muslin fabric, Jo-Ann Fabric

Hot glue gun

2-inch white satin ribbon, Michaels

Small doily, Jo-Ann Fabric

TO SEW THE BAGS

1 After figuring out how many bags and how much material you need, cut 2 pieces of linen to 6 × 7 inches (adjust size to make your bag smaller or larger). Stack them directly on top of each other, front sides facing.

2 Stitch three edges together, leaving one (usually a short side) open.

3 Turn the bag inside out and use your finger to push out the corners.

TO MAKE THE FLOWER DETAIL

4 Cut 4 pieces of muslin fabric to 6 × 6 inches, laying them on top of each other.

5 Fold the stack of muslin pieces in half.

6 Using your scissors, cut in a semicircle, making slight curves to create petals. Open the fabric and, piece by piece, layer it so that the petals face different directions.

7 Fold the fabric in half, then pinch in each side toward the center, holding tightly to the base, so that your muslin flower can lay flat.

8 Run your folded fabric flower, about ¼ inch from the tip (center of the flower), once through the sewing machine to secure the pieces together. Alternatively, you can tie a piece of twine tightly around the base of the flower. You might need two sets of hands to do this.

CONTINUED . . .

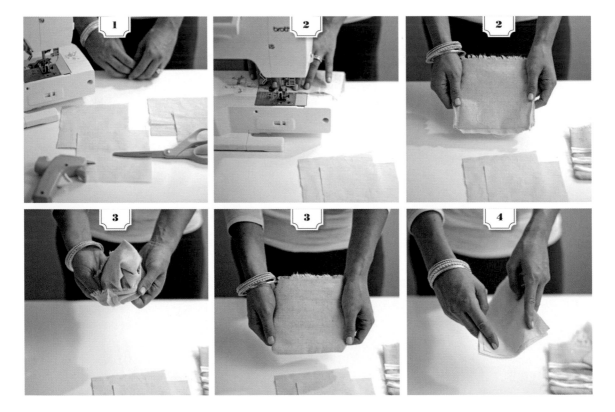

9 Using your glue gun, adhere the flower to the bag in the spot that you want, taking care not to let the glue seep through to the other side of the bag. You might need to hold the fabric up for a minute or two until dry.

10 Fluff your petals, twisting and lifting them so that they start to resemble a flower.

TO MAKE THE TWISTED RIBBON DETAIL

11 Cut four 8-inch pieces from the satin ribbon.

12 Twist the ribbon in a messy fashion, making sure that some parts are twisted tightly and others not at all. Don't worry too much about this step, as you can manipulate these as you are sewing them.

13 Place the top of the twisted ribbon on your sewing machine and begin sewing a straight line down the center. As you sew, manipulate the ribbon so that there are inconsistencies in how tightly it's twisted. Repeat with the remaining three strands.

14 Using your glue gun, adhere the strips about ½ inch apart at the base of your linen bag, taking care not to let the fabric stick to the backside of the bag. Trim the ribbon so that the edges line up to the sides of the bag.

A Blessing for STYLE-OBSESSED Brides Everywhere

SOMEONE ONCE TOLD ME that the weddings published on *Style Me Pretty* need to focus more on the love and less on the details of the day. To that I say . . . cheers.

Part of crafting and obsessing over flawless details means that you are infusing your wedding with love, with time spent among those you adore, glue gun in hand, laughing, dreaming, drinking copious amounts of wine or coffee depending on the hour, giddy about the day that is still months away and yet feels like tomorrow.

The ceremony, the words, the love, the romance, the passion, the first kiss . . . these are what make the foundation for a memorable wedding. The details—from the glitter-adorned vases to the handmade cake toppers and ombré napkins—are part of the greater story . . . the journey to building a day that is personal and wildly unique, a celebration of two individuals and all of their quirks in one beautiful moment.

Love and Details, my friends, are not mutually exclusive. If you allow them to walk hand in hand, your wedding will be nothing short of magic.

So go forth, you beautiful brides, you crafters of pretty. Embrace your inner style goddess and together with the ones you love, build yourself a day that overflows with personality, with uniqueness, and with pure joy.

Love, love, love . . . Abby

Credits

THE ANATOMY OF A BESPOKE WEDDING
Photography: Jose Villa Photography; cinematography: Nathan Pickett Films; event coordination: Joy Thigpen; floral and event design: Joy Thigpen; wholesale flowers: Fifty Flowers; invitation design: Rifle Paper Company; calligraphy: Plurabelle Calligraphy (Molly Suber Thorpe); vintage stamps: Verde Studio; map: Trial by Cupcakes (Laura Conduouris); cookie wedding favors: Cakes from Cabin Ridge; wedding cake: Cakes from Cabin Ridge; cake topper: Lollipop Workshop; catering: Zac's Montana Kitchen; bar service: Rocking K Bar; ceremony and reception venue: bride's family farm; officiant: Reverend Jan Witman; music: Capitol City DJs; furniture rentals: Celebrate Rentals and Strobel's Rentals; linens: La Tavola; transportation: Great Falls Historic Trolley; hair and makeup artist: Mar Romero of TEAM Hair and Makeup; wedding gown: Rosa Clara (modified by Nazzy Nazari); reception dress: Melissa Sweet Fiesole; bridal jewelry: Wilson (custom design); bride's shoes: Manolo Blahnik (ceremony), Jimmy Choo (reception), Hunter (Plan B Rain Boots); bridesmaids' dresses: Alfred Angelo; groom's attire: Paul Smith; groom's shoes: Paul Smith; groomsmen's apparel: Kohl's suits, Tie Bar ties

CLASSIC WEDDINGS

WHITE WEDDING PERFECTION
Photography: KT Merry; event and floral designer: Hutchinson's Floral Artistry; invitations and programs: Noteworthy By Design; custom print design: Courtney Callahan Paper; calligraphy: Calligraphy by Jennifer; cake: Betsy Irvin; catering: The Windsor; music: Element; rentals: Premier Party Rentals; lighting: Hutchinson's Floral Artistry; ceremony venue: The Windsor Chapel; reception venue: The Windsor; hair stylist: White Orchid Inn & Spa; makeup artist: Lena & Britta of Vero; wedding gown: Monique Lhuillier; bridesmaids' dresses: J. Crew; bridesmaids' earrings: Chan Luk; men's attire: Ermenegildo Zegna, John Varvatos; flower girl dresses: J. Crew

UNDERSTATED AND INSPIRED
Photography: Sarah Yates; event styling: Dandelion and Grey; wedding coordinator: Weddings by Melinda; floral design: three beans & co.; invitation design: The Groom;

catering: Huntington Catering; dessert bar: Sweet and Saucy; ceremony venue: St. Timothy Church; reception venue: SmogShoppe; music: DJ David Carvalho; rental: Archive Vintage Rentals and Antiquity Rentals; makeup and hair: Theresa Huang Makeup & Hair Design; wedding dress: Monique Lhuillier; reception dress: Notte by Marchesa; bridesmaids' dresses: H&M; groom's attire: Ben Sherman

ORGANIC ELEGANCE
Photography: Jen Huang Photography; cinematography: Kiss The Bride Films; event and floral designer: Crocus Hale; invitations and programs: Melangerie; cake: Something Sweet by Michelle; cake toppers: Creative Butterfly XOX; catering: Cranwell Resort; dessert bar: Cookie Creatives by Jennifer; favors: DIY; ceremony and reception venue: Cranwell Resort; officiant: Rabbi Dr. Terry R. Bard; music: Stardust Band; rentals and lighting: Crocus Hale; hair stylist: Jennifer Brent; makeup artist: Sergey Logvinov; wedding gown: Eli Saab for Pronovias; bridesmaids' dresses: Thread; bride's jewelry: Bergdorf Goodman; shoes: Michael Kors; men's attire: J. Crew and Paul Smith; groom's attire: Alton Lane; groom's tie: Ferragamo; chuzpah maker: Cassandra Holden.

MODERN WEDDINGS

ROOFTOP GARDEN CHIC
Photography: Shannon Renee Photography; cinematography: Jimmy Hammond; event planner: Abby LaDuke, Something Blue Wedding Company; event designer: Alison Montgomery, London West Hollywood Hotel; floral designer: Joji Rose Oliveros; cake and cupcakes: SusieCakes; cupcake packaging: DIY; catering: Gordon Ramsay Restaurant, London West Hollywood Hotel; ceremony and reception venue: The London West Hollywood Hotel; officiant: Alan Katz; string quartet: Fiddlestix; DJ: Angie Vee; lighting: Amber Event Production; hair stylist: Yuki Sharoni Salon; makeup artist: Astrid Reyes; wedding gown: Vera Wang; bride's jewelry: Tiffany & Co.; bride's shoes: Christian Louboutin; bridesmaids' necklaces: Me & Ro; bridesmaids' dresses: Nicole Miller; groom's attire: Ben Sherman

MODERN VINTAGE
Photography: Red Ribbon Studio; event coordinator: Samantha of Bellagala; floral designer: Le Jardin Floral; invitations: Mr. Boddington's Studio; cake and catering: D'Amico, Chambers Hotel; ceremony and reception venue: The Chambers Hotel; hair stylist: Guy Riggio for Sally Hershberger; wedding gown: Avion Feminin–Katherine Tsina; bridal jewelry: Erickson Beamon; bride's shoes: Lanvin; bridesmaids' dresses: Katherine Tsina, Avion Feminin; men's attire: J. Crew; groom's attire: Brooks Brothers

SOPHISTICATED LUXURY
Photography: Elizabeth Messina; cinematography: Fifty Foot Films; event planning: Lisa Vorce of Oh, How Charming; floral design: Mindy Rice Floral & Event Design; event design: Lisa Vorce and Mindy Rice; invitation design: Papel Paper & Press; cake: Vanilla Bake Shop; catering: The Sunset Tower Hotel; ceremony and reception venue: The Sunset Tower Hotel; ceremony music: Espi; reception music: James Gang of West Coast Music; rentals: Classic Party Rentals; specialty dance floor: Barker Décor Service; lighting: Barker Décor Service; hair stylist: Neil George; makeup artist: Heather Currie; wedding gown: Vera Wang; bride's shoes: Manolo Blahnik; bridesmaids' dresses: Badgley Mischka; groom's attire: Zegna

RUSTIC WEDDINGS

EFFORTLESS GRACE
Photography: Carrie Patterson; event planner and designer: Leah Chace of Jackson Hole Event Co.; floral designer: Lily & Co.; invitations design (including Save the Dates, wedding log, wedding brand, programs, and welcome letters): Mr. Boddington's Studio; calligraphy: Love, Jenna; cake: Jackson Cake Company; catering: Bistro Catering; ceremony: St. John's Episcopal Church; reception venue: Snake River Ranch; music: Sensations Soul; hair and makeup: Jamie Kramer of Beleza Salon; wedding gown: Peter Langner/Mark Ingram's Bridal Atelier; veil: Restored by Sewtique; bridesmaids' dresses: Valentino; men's ties: Peter-Blair

SWEET RUSTIC ROMANCE
Photography: Simply Bloom Photography; event designer: Proper Measures; desserts: Proper Measures; catering: Jim 'N Nicks Bar-B-Q; ceremony: The American Village Chapel; reception venue: The American Village; groom's attire: Banana Republic; music: Act of Congress; wedding gown: Melissa Sweet; bride's shoes: J. Renee

SUMMER CAMP CHARM
Photography: Kate Headley; cinematography: Well Spun Weddings; event planner and designer: Maria Cooke and Kelly Seizert of Ritzy Bee Events; floral designer: Holly Heider Chapple Flowers; invitation design: Simplesong Design; calligraphy: Meant to Be Calligraphy; pies: Chapple Farm; catering: Ken's Creative Kitchen; favors: Simplesong; ceremony and reception venue: Sherwood Forest; music: Evan Reitmeyer of My Deejay; rentals: Party Rental; transportation: Towne Transportation; makeup: Amie Decker Beauty; wedding gown: Blue by Enzoani; bridal jewelry: Nadri; bridesmaids' dresses: Simple Silhouettes; bridesmaids' necklaces: Miss Meri; bridesmaids' shoes: Butter; men's attire: Annapolis Formal Wear and Tuxedos; men's ties: Paul Fredrick

WHIMSICAL WEDDINGS

HANDCRAFTED GOODNESS
Photographers: Chris & Sarah Rhoads; event designer: the bride and her maid of honor, Lila Patil; wedding planner: the bride and bride's mother; day of coordination: J'adore Events; fabric chandelier: the bride and her parents; florist: Laurie at A New Leaf; invitation design and event signage: Katie Brooks; calligraphy: Love, Jenna; cupcakes: Sweet Mandy B's; catering: The Hearty Boys; officiant: Meghan Kennedy; ceremony and reception venue: A New Leaf; ceremony music (swing/jazz): John Kregor and Sam Macy; reception music: Dustin Drase of Toast & Jam; lighting and rentals: Deborah Weisenhaus of Art of Imagination; vintage photo booth: 312 Photobooth; hair: Vicki Tsafogiannis; makeup: Carley Martin; wedding gown: Carolina Herrera; bride's reception dress: 1950s vintage lace dress from Silver Moon Vintage; bride necklace: Dogeared Jewelry; earrings: Alexis Bittar; veil: Weddings 826; bridesmaids' dresses: BHLDN; groom's suit: Banana Republic; groom's tie: Neckties.com; groomsmen's ties: Rabbit Stop via Etsy

BLUSH-HUED PERFECTION

Photography: Charley*Star Photography; cinematography: Karen Wetterau; floral and event planner designer: Bash, Please; invitation design: Bash, Please; cake: SusieCakes; cake banners: Harriot Grace; favors: Bash, Please; catering: Town Hall Restaurant; ceremony and reception venue: private residence; officiant: Bill McAdam; music: Jason Aquino of DJ's & MC's; photo booth: Smile Booth; wedding gown: Mignon; bride's reception dress: Alice and Olivia; bride's shoes: Lanalia; jewelry: Cynthia Wolff; groom's attire: Brioni; flower girls' dresses: J. Crew

ANTIQUE CHIC

Photography: Erik Ekroth; event and floral designer: Hatch Creative Studio; event planner: Cristie Woodard of Plan-It Productions; invitation design: Dapper Paper Designs; cupcakes: Penelope NYC; catering: Neuman's Catering; music: Jim Roberti Band; ceremony and reception venue: Gary's Loft; officiant: Honorable Ira A. Pergament; hair stylists: Mike Viggue of Sally Hershberger Salon; makeup artist: Sam Murrell; wedding gown: Amsale; bride's shoes: Christian Louboutin; men's ties: Xoelle; groom's attire: Hugo Boss

CHARM DEFINED

Photographer: Sarah Yates; cinematographer: Floataway Studios; event planner and designer: Jesi Haack Design; florist: Honey and Poppies; invitation design: Dapper Paper; cake: Sweet and Saucy; catering: Huntington Catering; favors: bride; ceremony and reception venue: SmogShoppe; music: JP McLeod; photo booth: Phototastic; hair and makeup: ten.eleven makeup; wedding gown: La Sposa; bride's jewelry: BHLDN; bride's shoes: BHLDN; bridesmaids' dresses: J. Crew; bridesmaids' jewelry: Urban Outfitters and Anthropologie; groom's attire: J. Crew; menswear, groomsmen: Express

AL FRESCO WEDDINGS

EAST COAST LOVELY

Photography: Jen Huang Photography; cinematography: Mike Cyr of Buzz Media; floral design: Elements Flowers; invitation design: C'est Papier; Save the Date map: April Ink; cake: Vesta Bakery; catering: Shelter Harbor Golf Club; ceremony and reception venue: Shelter Harbor Golf Club; officiant: Rabbi Aaron Rosenberg; music: Original Faze 4 Orchestras; rentals: RI Rentals; tent and lighting: Exquisite Events; linens: Classic Party Rentals; hair stylist: Bella Vita; makeup artist: Cyndie Strawhecker; men's accessories: Paul Smith; wedding gown: Monique Lhuillier from Mark Ingram Bridal Salon; bride's shoes: Jimmy Choo; bridesmaids' dresses: Laundry by Shelli Segal; bridesmaids' shoes: Calvin Klein; groom's attire: Paul Smith

PRETTY IN PINK

Photography: Elizabeth Messina; cinematography: Living Cinema; event coordination: Alexandra Kolendrianos; floral and event design: Mindy Rice; invitation design: Lazaro Press and Design; printer: The Write Image; calligraphy: Ron Tate; cake and truffles: Bacara Resort & Spa; catering: Bacara Resort & Spa; ceremony and reception venue: Bacara Resort & Spa; officiant: Mark Majcen; music: Santa Barbara String Quartet and SB DJ's; furniture: Fusion Event Rentals; linens: La Tavola Linen; reception decor (fabric): Designing Life; rentals: Classic Party Rentals; photo booth: Capital Photobooths; lighting: Images By Lighting; transportation: Classy Chassis Rentals; hair stylist: Sheila Stone; makeup artist: Andrea Sutherland; wedding gown: Vera Wang; bridal jewelry: Adorn; bride's shoes: Badgley Mischka; bridesmaids' dresses: J. Crew; bridesmaids' shoes: Kelly & Katie; men's attire: Calvin Klein

WINE COUNTRY STYLE

Photography: Cooper Carras; event and floral designer: Megan Fickling of La Partie Events; event planner: Boutiquevents (bride); invitation design and calligraphy: BDUB NY; catering: Roblar Winery; cookie bar: Santini Millwork; cookies: Roblar Pastry; favors: Ordie & Chavalos; ceremony and reception venue: Roblar Winery; officiant: Tracy Dykes; music: The Brenna Whitaker Little Big Band; DJ: Canyon Cody; rentals: Classic Party Rentals; lighting and sound: SMI Concepts; hair and makeup: Mai Lookwood of Legends Salon; wedding gown: Cymbeline Paris in New York City; groom's attire: Umberto Autore

Thank-Yous

A QUICK NOTE OF GRATITUDE

for the people who made this project possible. First, to Claudia Ballard, our amazing agent, who saw the value in this book far before we did, who gave me permission to do things my way, to buck tradition, and who ensured that I was in the best hands possible. I adore you. To Aliza Fogelson and her pencil, who promised that the crazy passion in my brain would translate beautifully to the pages of this book. To Yumiko of Hana Floral Design in Stonington, Connecticut, SMP's floral guru. Thank you so very much for being our flower muse and identifying each stem used in every single wedding. You are loveliness defined. And to the girls of *Style Me Pretty*: For your eye, your support, and your constant devotion to this brand that together we have built, I heart you.

To my sweet mother, who has been editing my papers since I learned to write . . . who spent countless nights and the earliest of mornings helping to ensure that the words on these pages made sense, that my thoughts didn't get ahead of my fingers, and that her daughter stayed completely sane during the adventures of writing her first book. I love you more than I could ever express. And to my father, who drives me, who teaches me, who gives me permission to live every dream that I've ever had. And to live those very dreams with grace and integrity. Thank you.

And last but the furthest thing from least: To my husband, who holds my hand, who kisses me, who makes me feel like I'm the only girl in the world. To my spunky little girl, Audrey, who can make me laugh and cry at the exact same time. And my sweet boy, William, who is pure joy and yumminess. To my perfectly imperfect family, who gives me a reason to live this passion every single day.

STYLE TEAM FOR OUR BLUEPRINTS

Lisa Vorce. Dare I say Lisa is one of the best event stylists in the world? Yes, without a doubt. Lisa designs with a sense of creativity and style that pretty much goes unmatched. She approaches wedding design with care, with texture, with the idea that each piece, each moment is worthy of art. She is, in a word, genius.

Jose Villa. He is a photographer who is loved all around the world. He is gushed upon and e-obsessed over by bloggers and brides alike. But the best part of Jose? He lives up to every wonderful word that has been said about him. He is pure talent in its rawest form. He is soulful and layered, and that dimension shows through in every image. He is a friend and he is an inspiration to me every single day.

Kate Holdt. Kate is all loveliness. Kate designs flowers without rules, pulling together the most beautiful pieces a girl could ever want with a sense of effortless and laid-back elegance that invites the love. She blows me away time and time again, showing me that inspired design can be both approachable and totally chic at once.

Melody Brandon. She is the talent behind the beloved brand Sweet and Saucy Bakeshop, with designs that are "pinned" like none other. Her cakes are fashion. They are so utterly breathtaking, you can hardly imagine cutting into them. And just when you think she couldn't possibly create something more beautiful than what you've seen . . . she does. Over and over and over again. Melody is beyond.

Rebecca Schmidt Ruebensaal. Mr. Boddington, Rebecca's famed stationery and paper brand, is the place we go when we want to get really inspired. Rebecca's masterpieces have changed the invitation game entirely through designs that balance whimsy with formality, chicness with sweetness. Each and every collection that Rebecca crafts could be framed and used to grace the walls of even the most fabulous of homes. We heart Rebecca in a big way and are always on the edge of our seats to see what she comes up with next.

Index